THE CAT-A-LOGUE

Janice Anderson

GUINNESS BOOKS

Acknowledgements

The author wishes to thank the following people and organizations for providing information used in this book: Mrs P.A. Peters, the British Thematic Association, British Philatelic Federation; R.J. Webber, The Brewers' Society; The Cats Protection League; Governing Council of the Cat Fancy, for permission to reproduce details from the lists of Breed Numbers and the Standards of Points; *Guinness Book of Records* archives; National Cat Club (Mrs Grace Pond); Pet Food Manufacturers' Association; People's Dispensary for Sick Animals; The Post Office Archives; Potter's Museum of Curiosity; Victorian Paintings Department, Sotheby's, London; Syndication International for permission to reproduce *Weighing Bulgy* by William Connor (Cassandra); Publications Office, the Tate Gallery.

Cover pictures Bruce Coleman

Editor: Honor Head
Design and Layout: Michael Morey

Published in Great Britain by Guinness Superlatives Ltd,
33 London Road, Enfield, Middlesex

Typeset in 9/10 ITC Garamond Light
by D.P. Press Ltd, Sevenoaks, Kent.
Printed and bound in Portugal by Printer Portuguesa.

British Library Cataloguing in Publication Data

Anderson, Janice
The cat-a-logue. – 2nd ed
1. Cats. Stories, anecdotes
I. Title
636.8

ISBN 0–85112–328–7

This book has been a particular pleasure for Janice Anderson to write, since there has always been a much-loved pet cat or two in her family, starting off with the tiny, ginger Timothy, who had to be hastily rechristened Timmy when she produced three enchanting kittens. The present resident of the family cat box is another ginger mog, Angus, pictured here helping the author with some of the finer points of 'The Cat-a-logue'.

Words have been Janice Anderson's business all her life, starting with a junior reporter's job on her local daily paper in Christchurch, New Zealand, where she was born, and progressing through a period as assistant press officer at the Save the Children Fund's London headquarters and a much longer period as editor in a large London publishing house. Today, she is a freelance writer, specialising in travel and movie books, though she has also had published books on various non-fiction subjects, including social history.

She lives in Marlow, Buckinghamshire, with her husband, travel writer Edmund Swinglehurst, and son Nicholas.

Contents

Cats and Us 7

The Inimitable Cat 31

The Pedigree Cat 51

The Cat in the Language 74

Cats in the Arts 91

Cult of the Cat 115

An Egyptian tomb drawing shows that cats have been domesticated since 2,600 BC.

Cats and Us

The cat is a fairly late comer to domesticity; even now, the cat is not fully domesticated, being far more independent than other 'domestic' animals. Cats may have thrown in their lot with man, as far as they have done so at all, about 5,000 years ago, compared with the dog's 10,000 years, though some experts would put the date over a thousand years more recent than that.

Cat genealogy

The cat who sits purring on our laps can trace his ancestry back more than 13 million years to a small, weasel-like carnivorous creature called *Miacis*. From this pre-historic animal descended such animals as the dog, raccoon, hyena and civet as well as our cat, which descended from *Miacis* via a branch which evolved into the first truly cat-like animal, *Ditictis*.

All domestic cats come within one species, called *F. catus*, of the family *Felidae*, the other 37 species of which are all wild cats, great and small. The cat's closest relations today are the African Wild Cat (*Felis libyca*) and the European Wild Cat (*Felis sylvestris*), with both of which the domestic cat may breed. No wonder the poet Samuel Taylor Coleridge remarked that when he stroked his little cat he 'felt closest to the tiger'.

Cats in history

An **Egyptian tomb drawing** dating back to the fifth dynasty (*c.* 2,600 BC) and depicting a cat with a wide collar round its neck, indicates that cats, albeit wild cats as this one may have been, have been put to use by man for 4,500 years.

In 529 BC **Cambyses of Persia** conquered Egypt and had himself crowned king. During his campaign of conquest the king is said to have used cats against the cat-loving and superstitious Egyptians. He issued his soldiers with cats and the Egyptians and their King Psammeticus III, terrified of harming the animals, allowed the Persian army to take the city of Pelasium without a blow being struck.

The ancient cities of **Carthage** and **Alexandra** each had cat populations estimated at more than 100,000 strong.

The **Phoenicians**, who traded tin ore with Cornish tin miners, are known to have brought cats to the British Isles, bartering them for the precious ore. The **Romans**, too, probably brought domestic cats with them. The bones of cats have been found in the burnt-out ruins of Roman villas.

The accidental death of a cat, killed in Egypt by a Roman soldier who was lynched by an angry crowd of cat-loving Egyptians, is said to have helped spark off the war between **Rome and Egypt** which ended only with the deaths of **Antony** and **Cleopatra** after the Battle of Actium.

The first cat breeding plan was established in **Japan** in AD 999. Though the date may be more legend than fact, it seems certain that around that time at the Emperor's court at Kyoto five pure white kittens were born to a white cat imported from China. The kittens were born on the tenth day of the fifth moon, which seemed such a good omen that the Emperor ordered that the cats should be specially cared for and allowed to breed only with each other. Cats instantly became fashionable pets in Japan.

One of the worst cat massacres unconnected with religious superstition was that which occurred in **Paris** in the 1730s when printing apprentices tortured and ritually slaughtered as many cats as they could find. The massacre began as an oblique attack by a group of printing apprentices against their master and his wife, who had a pet cat of which she was inordinately fond, but turned into a fierce protest against social conditions in Paris at the time.

The cat did not always fare much better in **England** in the 18th century. At this period visitors to the centuries-old menagerie in the

Revered in Ancient Egypt, cats were mummified before they were buried.

Tower of London could either pay threepence to get in to see the animals or provide a dog or cat to be fed to the lions.

The first domestic cats to reach **North America** were brought by a French missionary who gave a fine pair of French ratters to a chief of the **Huron Indians.** The Indians, not knowing what to do with these animals, left them to their own devices and they died without producing kittens. It was not until 1749 that a conscious decision was taken to import cats into the colonies on the American East Coast seaboard, largely to help control plagues of black rats.

One of the most notorious, if unwitting, acts of grave robbery in history occured at **Beni Hassan** in **Egypt** in 1888 when an ignorant farmer dug up an Ancient Egyptian cat necropolis containing thousands of carefully mummified cats and even a few mice embalmed for cat food in the next world. Because of the vast amount of cat mummies rescued, the majority were sold as fertilizer. However some went to museums and provided Egyptologists with most of the information we have about Ancient Egyptians and their cats.

Cat calling

If a survey carried out by the British Market Research Bureau for Spillers Top Cat in 1981 is anything to go by, most British cats are called by rather pedestrian and predictable names. Sooty turned out to be the most popular name for British cats, with Smoky, Brandy, Fluffy and Tiger not far behind. The survey did uncover some more adventurous names, however, including Japonica, Troggs, Lydia la Poose, Serapham Simkin, Hosanna and Henderson.

Beppo was the name chosen by two poets, **Lord Byron** and **Jorge Luis Borges**, for their cats. Beppo (short for Guiseppe) was the eponymous hero of one of Byron's poems; a Venetian taken captive in Troy, he turned Turk and joined a band of pirates, with whom he became rich and successful.

The full name of **Samuel Taylor Coleridge**'s cat **Rumpel** was **The Most Noble the Archduke Rumperstilzchen, Marcus Macbum, Earl Tomnefuagne, Baron Raticide, Waowhler and Scratch**.

Among **Cardinal Richelieu**'s many cats were **Lucifer** (a black Angora), **Gazette**, **Soumise**, **Thisbe**, **Rubis**, **Pyrame**, **Rita**, **Perruque** and **Racan**. The last two were so named because they were born in the wig of the Marquis de Racan.

Queen Victoria's love for Scotland no doubt prompted her to call her cherished white Persian **White Heather**.

H.G. Wells called his cat **Mr Peter Wells**; **Victor Hugo** called his **Gavroche**; and **Theophile Gautier**, **Mde Theophile**.

Little prescience was shown in the naming of the cat considered to be the greatest Black Longhair of all time, **Dirty Dick**, who was born in 1911, won 14 championships and sired many outstanding kittens. Entrants in the Black Longhaired section of the 89th National Cat Club Show at Olympia, London, in 1985 were more grandly named:

Aduelo Black Benson, **Ch. Samouti Black Carlos**, **Lochmoy Black Macian** and **Ch. Elvenwake Damion**, for instance.

Some of the outstanding names of the winners in the 1986 show include the following:

Fluffeline Blue Yeoman
Jocolue Rosy Posy
Ch. Scotchmist Stanley
Bonzeta Fairy Queen
Ch. Millcoombe Painted Lady
Ch. Panns Pollydoodle
Headway Rambo
Adreelo Sunshine Girl
Sapajou Pastel Portrait
Ch. Pallisand Cudley Dudley
Ch. Anneby Ragamuffin
Quartet Rockabye Baby
Ch. Mockorange Big Boy
Apalachee Sitting Bull
Apalachee Laughing Water
Ch. Honeymist Marianna
Purrfun My Main Man
Elvenwake Montgomery
Millcoombe Golly Gosh
Brambleberry Sapper
Doleygate Dignified
Cooperleaf Candy
Snowfleet Firefly
Chrysellus Cream Flashman
Skipmandu Snow Bird
Raindance No Surrender
Skipmandu Mix 'N' Match
Myrazz Dolly Mixture
Deanview Silver Sudamach
Treadaway Fergie
Larkswood Cuckoo
Adqwelo Pastel Delight
Honeycharm Amanda
Alzab April Fool
Zibarque Toger Tots
Ch. Pr Cacharel Ragamuffin Rafels
Fynmile Red Hot Lover
Gr. Pr Honeycharm Autumn Dawn
Pr Glamourpuss Cream Teddy
Ch. Satinmist August Moon
Gr. Ch. Satinmist Summer Magic
Cobbychops Chatsworth
Sheephouse Bopeep
Sheephouse Little Posey
Tinkerbelle Painted Lady
Cyanmist Sugar Plum
Pennydown Jubilee Jasper
Porteous Heathcliff
Mycene Amber Glow
Syringa Black Orchid
Heatherslade Henrietta
Elfinstar Lilac Shadow
Keiko Texas Tycoon
Seeteez Black Enthusiast
Sisophon Salamander
Moonstruck Lylac Tyger
Antiquity Troopingcolor
Rumba Edelweiss
Mousepolice Charlie
Gr. Pr. Kizwozzi Mister Softie
Ch. Cherubin Sweet Kandida
Ch. Moonswift Lady Masumi
Ch. Shomiro Silver Dollar
Justafancie Belle Lydia
Balsia Bertiewoosta
(*Gr. Pr = Grand Premier*)

T.S. Eliot, author of *Old Possum's book of Practical Cats*, may well have based this wonderfully entertaining collection of cats on some of his own. During his life he had many cats, giving them such names as **Wiscus**, **Pattipaws** and **George Pushdragon**, this last name being the pseudonym the poet used when he entered crossword competitions in *Time and Tide* magazine. To judge by his poem, *The Naming of Cats*, Eliot considered that a cat must have three names – an everyday name, such as 'Peter', a more 'particular', 'dignified' name, such as 'Quaxo', 'Bombalurina' or 'Jellylorum' and thirdly the name the cat thinks up for himself, his 'deep and inscrutable singular Name'.

Sir Roy Strong, former Director of London's Victoria and Albert

The Reverend Wenceslas Muff by Martin Leman.

Museum, calls his handsome black-haired, golden-eyed cat **The Reverend Wenceslas Muff**. For a time, visitors to the museum could buy a poster of the Director and his pet.

Fat cats

To the average person in a third world country, most cats kept as pets in the western world must seem 'fat cats': according to statistics published in 1986, the money spent on the average contented western cat's upkeep – about £170 a year – is greater than the per capita gross national product of the people who live in the world's 15 poorest countries. Even so, some western world pussy cats are 'fatter' than others, having landed on their feet in surroundings rich even by our standards.

Cardinal Richelieu, ruler of France in all but name from 1629 until his death in 1642, kept dozens of cats at the French Court for all of which he had a near-fanatical affection. He left pensions to 14 of his cats in his will, and made provision for two guardians to be paid to look after them. The poor creatures hardly had time to enjoy their pensions for Swiss mercenaries at the court broke into the cats' apartments, butchered all of them and turned them into a huge stew.

Katherine Tofts, a soprano who made a fortune during her short but brilliant career on the London opera stage, retiring in 1709 when she was about 30, left legacies in her will to 20 cats when she died in 1758. Wrote 'Peter Pindar', the popular satirist of the day:

'Not Niobe mourned more for fourteen brats,
Nor Mistress Tofts, to leave her twenty cats.'

The cat of another musician, Mademoiselle Dupuy, did not do so well. Mlle Dupuy attributed her skill as a harpist to her cat's critical appreciation of her playing and marked her gratitude for this by leaving him in her will two houses and an income large enough to support both. Her family contested the will and had it revoked.

Another great figure of the age to leave annuities in her will for her cats was the Duchess of Richmond, one-time mistress of Charles II. This inspired Alexander Pope to write the famous waspish couplet in his *Moral Essays:*

'But thousands die without this or that,
Die, and endow a college or cat.'

When Philip Stanhope, 4th Earl of Chesterfield, the English statesman and man of letters, died in 1773, leaving handsome pensions to all his cats in his will, he was following a precedent set by another English aristocrat, the 2nd Duke of Montagu. When His Grace died in 1749 it was found that he had added a codicil to his will in favour of his pets, which included many cats.

The richest cat heirs on record were two 15-year-olds, Hellcat and Brownie, who were left $415,000

out of the estate of their owner, Dr William Grier, of San Diego, California, USA in the early 1960s.

Even better off, because he had the whole bequest to himself, was an impressive white alley cat, Charlie Chan, who was left the entire estate of his owner, Mrs Grace Alma Patterson of Joplin, Missouri, USA, on her death in 1978. The estate, which included a three-bedroom house, a seven-acre pet cemetary and a valuable antiques collection, was worth about $250,000.

1988 was a good year for bequests to cats in Britain. First, Mrs Dorothy Walker of Richmond, Surrey, left £2,767,752 to the RSPCA, on condition that the Society look after her cat, Pussy. Then came the announcement that Mr Ben Rea, a retired antiques dealer from Taplow in Berkshire, had died, leaving 'several million pounds' to three cat charities.

Britain's richest cat, Blackie, inherited his owner's estate on similar conditions to Charlie Chan. Mrs Ivy Blackhurst died in 1975, directing in her will that Blackie should continue to live in her house in Sheffield and enjoy all the benefits of her estate, valued then at around £35,000; on Blackie's death the residue of the estate was to go to the RSPCA (Royal Society for the Prevention of Cruelty to Animals). Alas, inflation caught up with Blackie and his house had to be sold. The proceeds were put into a trust for him and Blackie moved into a cattery where he lived until his death in 1978.

In 1983 a retired British Rail clerk, Mr Harry Stevelman, left all his money, about £65,000, for his five cats, Suki, Tessa, Pippa, Ginger and Gemma, to be looked after.

And in 1984, two English ladies made valuable bequests to friends, on condition that they looked after the ladies' cats. Mrs Marie Bretherton had had 20 cats at one time, but at her death her 'family' was down to eight, so that her old friend, retired dustman Charlie Pritchard, felt that he could easily cope with her bequest: £72,000 to keep her cats in the manner to which they had become accustomed. Miss Margaret Tribble was perhaps less fortunate, for she was left £20,000 in the will of Miss Madeleine Battersby, on condition that she look after Miss Battersby's 20 cats.

Meanwhile, back in America, some 125 cats were enjoying the hospitality of Standard Oil heiress, Patricia Ladew, who had decided in 1981 to be really practical about her work for stray cats. She bought a $100,000, two-storey house especially for them in fashionable Oyster Bay, New York. This home for homeless cats came complete with live-in servants, radios for the cats' listening pleasure and tables and chairs covered in small carpets for them to scratch satisfactorily, all at Mrs Ladew's expense.

The small town of Pitman, New Jersey, found itself the centre of attention in the USA in 1986 when its borough council passed an historic edict limiting to three the number of cats any householder could 'keep, harbour or maintain'. The council had had complaints about people keeping 10 or 12 cats and not looking after them properly; the local board of health showed no sign of doing anything, so the council introduced its law. There was instant uproar among

the nation's seriously ruffled cat-lovers and the media descended on the town in force to investigate its cats.

'This town is officially listed as having the Number One toxic waste site in the entire United States; we've got a contaminated lake here which contains all the known cancer-causing agents there are,' said the Mayor, who had been trying unsuccessfully to attract the media's attention to this problem waste site for years. 'Now they're all here because of the cats.'

The financial pulling power of cats, even poetical ones, should never be underestimated. When Andrew Lloyd Webber fulfilled a long-held ambition and turned T.S. Eliot's *Practical Cats* into the heroes of a rock musical called *Cats* in 1981, he sent the Jellicle Cats, the Old Gumbie Cat, Grizabella, Skimbleshanks and the rest into a financial spin. In 1985 the *Financial Times* newspaper published a report that in the year before the musical had earned Eliot's publishers, Faber & Faber, £650,000 in royalties and was expected to earn twice that much in 1985. Since *Cats* was in production in 11 cities around the world in January 1986 and had netted $2 million in the USA alone in 1985, that looks like a very conservative estimate, especially when one knows that at the time of the public flotation of Lloyd Webber's company, the Really Useful Group in 1986, 90 per cent of its forecast profits of £4.2 million derived from *Cats*.

Cats and the courts

The **9th-century King Henry I of Saxony** decreed that the fine for killing a cat should be 60 bushels of corn.

In **936 Prince Howell the Good of Wales** caused a long and detailed law to be enacted concerning the value of a cat. It set the price of a new-born kitten at one penny rising to twopence once the kitten had proved its ability to kill a mouse and to fourpence (the value of a lamb) when it reached hunting age making the cat a valuable animal indeed. Another section of the law ordered that a man who killed or stole a cat should recompense the owner with as much wheat as would completely cover the animal when it was held up by the tail with its nose touching the ground.

In **1624**, during **Charles I**'s reign, an English court ruled that a person could not be expected in normal circumstances to keep his cat within the confines of his property, pointing out that 'It is the common usage of mankind to allow them wider liberty.'

From our own time comes the historic reasoning of American statesman **Adlai Stevenson** in vetoing a bill of the Illinois state legislature in **1949**. The bill sought to 'provide protection to insectivorous birds by restraining cats'. Stevenson, then Governor of Illinois, returned the bill, unapproved, because, he wrote: 'I cannot agree that it should be the declared public policy of Illinois that a cat visiting a neighbour's yard or crossing the public highways is a public nuisance. It is the nature of cats to do a certain amount of unescorted roaming. The State of Illinois and its governing bodies have enough to do without trying to control feline delinquency.

A scene from 'Cats'.

The rarified world of the English cat show became the background of a court-room argument about ownership as early as **1898**. Two women who jointly owned a champion Persian cat called **Roy**, one of them putting up the money to buy the cat, and the other paying for his food and upkeep, found their partnership falling apart. When he had been entered in a National Cat Club Show at Crystal Palace, where he had won several prizes and a championship medal, Roy had both ladies' names as owners on his entry form. But soon after the Crystal Palace successes, one of the women said that Roy, and his prizes, were hers, and even entered Roy in another cat show as her cat entirely. Her erstwhile partner went to court to establish legally her share in Roy – and won.

In **1984** a handsome marmalade tom, **Marmaduke Gingerbits**, filled many column inches in British newspapers when he was the centre of a nine-month-long legal ownership wrangle, the cost of which reached a surprising £7,000. Marmaduke Gingerbits had no valuable pedigree to spur his rightful owners into battle. Police Constable John Sewell and his wife Anna, having had their right to possession of Marmaduke Gingerbits confirmed by the Bow County Court Registrar, said they had fought the good fight simply for love of their pet.

Of even greater interest to the British public at large, because a genuine feline television star was involved, was the **1968–69** English court battle concerning the ownership of **Arthur**, an impressive white short-hair who appeared in a long-running series of television advertisements eating a well-known brand of catfood by scooping it out of the can with his left paw. Spillers, the pet-food manufacturer, obtained a legal judgment that they were the owners of Arthur, having bought him for £1,000 from Mr Toneye Manning. Mr Manning, an actor, not only refused to give up Arthur to Spillers but said that Spillers had been ill-treating Arthur by having his teeth extracted so he had to eat with his paw. The Court asked to see Arthur to check this and Mr Manning refused, saying that Arthur was beyond the jurisdiction of the British courts, and said the cat was in the Russian Embassy. The Embassy, incensed at being dragged into a *cause célèbre* about a cat, denied this emphatically. Arthur eventually turned up on a doorstep in West Hampstead (with all his teeth intact) providing a Fleet Street journalist with a splendid scoop, newspaper readers with a lot of fun, and Mr Manning with a great deal of publicity – and a spell in prison for contempt of court for having refused to give up the cat.

The way a cat plays with a mouse before killing it, lay behind the popular name for an anti-suffragette Act of Parliament. The **'Cat and Mouse Act'** was the Prisoners (Temporary Discharge for Ill-health) Act of **1913**, passed at the height of the Suffragettes' campaign in Britain before World War I. The act was aimed at preventing any of the women in the movement achieving martyrdom during hunger strikes in prison: women ill from hunger could be released on licence, and could be re-arrested if necessary.

THE CAT AND MOUSE ACT

PASSED BY THE LIBERAL GOVERNMENT

WSPU

THE LIBERAL CAT

ELECTORS VOTE AGAINST HIM!

KEEP THE LIBERAL OUT!

BUY AND READ 'THE SUFFRAGETTE' PRICE 1D.

A poster graphically illustrates the 'brutality' of the anti-suffragette act passed by the Government in 1913.

There have been a few interesting court cases in the United States of America, too, some of them detailed by Mrs Muriel Beadle in her authoritative book *The Cat: History, Biology and Behavior* (Simon & Schuster, New York; Collins/Harvell, U.K. 1977). A case which established the cat as a piece of valuable property was heard in Maine in **1914**. Mr Carl Thurston's fox hound tried to kill Mr Alonzo Carter's cat, on Mr Carter's land. Mr Carter shot the dog, and Mr Thurston sued for damages for its loss. The court found against Mr Thurston, on the grounds that American common law held that a dog 'found worrying, wounding or killing any domestic animal . . . outside of the inclosure or immediate care of its owner or keeper' could be lawfully killed. Mr Thurston took the case to Maine's Superior Court, arguing that the cat was not a domestic animal. Again he lost, the court ruling that cats *were* domestic animals and that they may be 'properly considered things of value'.

The case of Teresa Bischoff versus G. Leroy Cheney in the Connecticut courts, also in **1914**, highlighted the difficulty of accusing a cat of trespassing. Ms Bischoff sued Mr Cheney for damages because his Angora cat had trespassed on her property and bitten her. She lost because, the court ruled, 'the practical impossibility of preventing a cat trespassing, the infrequency of damage from its wanderings, and the freedom to roam permitted it by all, makes especially reasonable the rule that no negligence can be attributed to the mere trespass of a cat which has neither mischievous nor vicious propensities'.

In **1985** Judge Robert F. Gammon of the Small Claims Court in Lawrence, Indiana, brought in a stray cat, which he called **Court Cat**, to help clear his court of mice. Before setting Court Cat to work, Gammon took him to the vet to be neutered and to have all the injections a cat should have; then he bought it food and a litter box. Finally, he claimed $172 on his official expenses claim for all this.

The state auditor ruled that Judge Gammon had 'improperly spent the $172' and would not allow his claim. 'It's another case of bureaucracy running wild,' an incensed Judge Gammon is reported to have said, before appealing against the auditor's ruling, pointing out Court Cat's effectiveness in ridding his court of mice. After some time, Judge Gammon received a reply from the State Board of Accounts: 'After in-depth consideration, we have now decided to allow your expenditure.' Court Cat was still on the job as official mouser in 1986.

Cat people

Many people who have left their mark on history have enjoyed the companionship of cats. They have not done so for the sake of the ego-massage offered by the regard of a devoted animal – 'To his dog, every man is Napoleon, hence the popularity of dogs,' quipped Aldous Huxley in cynical mood – but rather for the fact, noted by Konrad Lorenz, that 'the cat is not really a domestic animal and his chief charm lies in the fact that . . . he still walks by himself". Perhaps people in the public eye need the self-possessed companionship of their cats as a route back down to everyday reality where no man is so important that a cat will fawn before him.' As the often quoted remark by Montaigne about his cat has it, 'I don't know if she is playing with me, or I am playing with her.'

CULTURAL CATS

Every schoolboy knows that **Samuel Johnson** fed his cat, **Hodge**, oysters. The great and good Doctor bought the oysters himself lest the servants, put to a lot of trouble for a cat, might take against the 'poor creature'. James Boswell recorded Johnson playing with his cat. Hodge was 'one day scrambling up Dr Johnson's breast, apparently with much satisfaction, while my friend, smiling and half whistling, rubbed down his back and pulled him by the tail; and when I observed he was a fine cat, saying 'Why, yes, Sir, but I have had cats whom I liked better than this;' and then, as if perceiving Hodge to be out of countenance, adding, 'but he is a very fine cat, a very fine cat, indeed'.

When telling this anecdote about Doctor Johnson and Hodge Boswell, who was allergic to cats, added 'I am, unluckily, one of those who have an antipathy to a cat, so that I am uneasy when in a room with one; and, I own, I frequently suffered a good deal from the presence of . . . Hodge.'

The **Brontës of Haworth** generally had a pet cat or two about them. Charlotte, in a letter, and

Painting by Emily Brontë of Keeper, her dog, and unnamed family cat.

Pencil drawing of a cat by Patrick Branwell Brontë.

Sir Walter Scott with his beloved cat, Hinx, by Sir John Watson Gordon.

Emily, in her diary, both mentioned with sadness the death of 'our poor little cat' Tiger in 1844. Emily devoted one of a series of essays she wrote in French to the cat. 'I can say with sincerity that I like cats,' she wrote firmly. 'A cat is an animal which has more human feelings than almost any other . . .'

Among writers who have worked best with cats sitting near at hand have been **Sir Walter Scott**, who had his portrait painted with his cat Hinx beside him; **Edgar Allan Poe**, who often worked with his cat sitting on his shoulder, **Colette**, **Emile Zola**, **Ernest Hemingway**, **and the historian A.L. Rowse**.

Lord Byron, who may have had a cat by him as he worked, certainly had them when he travelled; 'ten horses, eight enormous dogs, five cats, an eagle, a crow and a falcon' were counted in his mobile menagerie by one observer.

So devoted to the cat was the French writer **Colette** that not only was she frequently photographed with a cat in her arms or sitting among the work on her desk, but she once even appeared on stage miming 'La Chatte Amoureuse'. A photograph of her posing as the Sphynx is famous. The first of her books to be published under her own name, rather than that of her husband, Willy, was *Dialogues des Bètes* (1904), which was a small collection of conversations between her Angora cat, Kiki-la-Doucette, and her French bulldog, Toby-Chien. Her famous story, *La Chatte* (1933), in which a young bride had to compete with her husband's cat for his love, only to lose, had as model for the cat her own beloved 'guardian angel' Saha. Colette once remarked that 'our perfect companions' never have fewer than four feet'.

Colette's love for cats was in a fine French tradition. Among French writers enamoured of cats have been **Victor Hugo**, **Baudelaire**, **Mallarme**, **Gautier** and **Champfleury** whose book *Les Chats* (1868) was produced in a de luxe edition with illustrations by Manet.

Detective-story writer **Raymond Chandler** called his black Persian Taki his 'feline secretary'. She would sit on his manuscripts as he was trying to revise them, putting some of the pages out of reach of the writer's pen.

Domenico Scarlatti's cat is said to have suggested the outline for a sonata, known now as the *Cat's Fugue*, when it walked up and down the keyboard of the composer's harpsichord. Even though it is likely that it was simply the arrangements of the notes that suggested the name, playwright Peter Schaffer gave the story some authority by putting it in the mouth of Salieri, leading character in his play *Amadeus*.

Albert Schweitzer was another who would allow his cat to influence his writing work. The left-handed Schweitzer often chose to struggle on with the pen in his right hand rather than disturb his pet Sizi, who liked to sleep on his left arm.

RELIGIOUS CATS

When the prophet **Mohammed**'s cat fell asleep on the long sleeve of his robe, Mohammed, called to prayer, cut the sleeve off rather than wake the cat. There is a corollary to this story: in Tunis, they say that cats always turn towards Mecca when performing their ablutions.

Gregory I, the Great, who was consecrated pope in 590 and was canonised after his death, at one stage in his life withdrew for a time into a monastery, having given all his wealth to the poor, and took with him as his only companion a cat.

Henry VIII's Chancellor, **Cardinal Wolsey**, took his cat to religious services and to council meetings.

The 19th-century **Pope Leo XII** cherished a cat called Michetto, which had been born in the Raphael Loggia of the Vatican, and which the Pope often had by his side when he gave audiences.

ARMY CATS

Military men have not only loved cats but recognised their uses, too.

General Eliot, who commanded the garrison on the Rock of Gibraltar during the siege of 1779–80, looked only for companionship in his cat when he permitted her to accompany him on his daily tour of inspection, prancing happily and oblivious of the artillery fire.

Frederick the Great, while he apparently preferred the company of his spoilt Italian greyhounds, certainly knew the worth of cats; he ordered hundreds of them to be obtained to guard his army's stores depots.

The French politician **Colbert** used cats for a similar purpose, this time ordering three or four of them to be kept on every ship of the French navy.

STATELY CATS

There have been numerous statesmen well-known for their devotion to their cats. One of **Theodore Roosevelt**'s cats, Slippers, was so sure of his own importance in the world that he once flopped down in the hall mid-way between the White House's state drawing room and dining room, making all the important guests at that evening's state dinner walk round him. Another of **Roosevelt**'s cats, Tom Quartz, had his biography published.

In France, at about the same time, the Prime Minister, Georges Clemenceau, had a splendid Blue Persian at the Elysée Palace.

Winston Churchill's ginger tom, Jock, generally slept on his master's bed and attended many war-time cabinet meetings.

A cat fight at Number 10 Downing Street made a footnote in British Government history in 1967 during the prime ministership of **Harold Wilson**. **Mrs Wilson**, in trying to separate her Siamese, Nemo, from a black-and-white stray mog attacking him, received a scratch which turned septic, causing her to miss an official dinner party for the Italian Prime Minister, Sr Aldo Moro.

ROYAL CATS

There have been royal cat fans in the past, including Louis XV's **Queen Marie Leczinska** and **Queen Victoria**, but among today's British royal family, famous for their love of dogs, there have been very few cat owners, and cats are seldom to be seen in royal households. An exception is **Princess Michael of Kent**; she is the only member of the present Royal Family to have issued an official photograph including a cat, in this case her pet Siamese.

CATALLERGY

Some people do not just dislike cats; they may be psychologically very distressed by them, or be physically allergic to them, particularly their fur. (There have even been instances of cats being allergic to their own fur!)

Several military heroes, apparently fearless in battle, have been reduced to quivering horror at the sight of a cat. **Julius Caesar** was one such, and so was **Napoleon Bonaparte**. Once, when the latter was on campaign, one evening in his quarters he suddenly began shouting loudly for help. An aide, rushing in, found the great general, sword in hand, eyes starting from his head, confronting – a small kitten.

While the great British Afghan, Indian and Boer War general, **Lord Roberts VC**, did not dislike cats, he was certainly allergic to them, and would start to sneeze if he so much as found himself in the same room as a cat.

William Shakespeare may have had the same problem. The man who had Shylock, in *The Merchant of Venice*, saying 'Some . . . are mad if they behold a cat . . . a harmless necessary cat,' is said to have been allergic to them, leaving a room if he found a cat in it.

General **Dwight D. Eisenhower**, leading World War II general and president of the United States, did not hide his dislike of cats, issuing orders to the staff of his Gettysburg home that any cats seen in the grounds were to be shot.

The composer **Johannes Brahms** went further: he is said to have done the shooting himself, with a bow and arrow from an open window.

Nor have rulers been immune from this strange malady. **Henry III** of France *and* his brother, **Charles IX**, actually fell into a swoon if a cat came near them, and a **Grand Sultan of Turkey**, **Abdul Hamid**, felt overwhelming terror at the sight of a cat.

Cat crazy

Though few would go as far as **Edward Lear** (whose devotion to his cat Foss caused him when moving from one villa to another in San Remo to have the second built as an exact replica of the first so that Foss would not be inconvenienced by the move) there have been people who have

Foss, adored cat of Edward Lear.

been motivated by their liking, and sometimes dislike, for cats, to do some extraordinary things.

In 1967 *The Guardian* newspaper reported that a Frenchwoman, **Mde Olga Courtois**, had put her dead 19-year-old black and white cat, Chouquette, into the deep freeze. The cat, who had the freezer to herself, was laid on a blue embroidered cushion under a linen sheet and with flowers around her. Mde Courtois was awaiting the day when medical science would have advanced sufficiently to restore Chouquette to life.

The **17th-century Doge of Venice**, the great warrior, **Francesco Mori**, was said to love only his cat, who accompanied Mori on his campaigns, where he might be seen on the poop of the Doge's ship or in his campaign tent. When the cat died, the Doge kept his skeleton like some holy relic.

An American manufacturer, Pet Medical and Health Products of Princeton, New Jersey, has developed a mouthwash for cats and dogs with bad breath. The mouthwash comes in a pump-spray bottle and has in it bacteria killing agents and plaque reducers. The company reported that pets on which it had been tested did not seem to mind it and instinctively licked their lips to spread it around their mouths.

The pillar of the Chinchilla stud book was **Silver Lambkin**, rather inappropriately named considering his great size, enormous frill and advanced age when he died (17). After his death Silver Lambkin was stuffed and put on show in the Natural History Museum in London.

Hotel owner, **John Hall**, has seven charming cats in his hotel in Wabasha, Minnesota. He offers them, with the compliments of the management, as friendly companions for his guests during their stay. The staff of cats is headed by a grandfather, Morris, a half-Siamese weighing in at 30 lb (14 kg). Mr Hall says his cats are in use 99 per cent of the time.

A man whose neighbour in Tilbourg, the Netherlands, fed 21 noisy cats every night at around 2.30 a.m., eventually went berserk and stormed his neighbour's house with a pick axe. The police arrived as he was pounding holes in a wall.

Mrs Jane Reynolds and her husband retired to Majorca for a quiet life some 35 years ago. Today, the 84-year-old Englishwoman works all hours of the day, seven days a week looking after as many as possible of the thousands of stray and desperately ill-treated cats and dogs on the island. Her animal sanctuary, Centro Carino Internacional, Calle Jesus, Palma usually has about 300 in residence, and it costs her £2,500 a month to keep the place going. To raise the

money she organises bazaars and jumble sales and writes a weekly column in Majorca's English-language newspaper, the *Daily Bulletin*, to draw in donations. She has also built up a world-wide list of members, whose regular donations to the Centro Carino help keep it in funds.

An **English couple on holiday in the Algarve**, Portugal, in 1984 met a stray young cat. It was a case of love at first sight for all three, and the couple decided to bring the cat back to England. There were import documents to obtain, transport to arrange, quarantine regulations to meet . . . The additional costs on the couple's package holiday totalled £1,000.

A late 1981 *Time* magazine report on the cat craze in the **United States** noted the following items available for pampered American pets: Kitty Whiz, a potty trainer intended to teach Puss to use the bathroom lavatory; The Cat-A-Lac rolling bed (a snip at $34); a rocking horse to calm 'the freaked-out feline'; a kitty water bed; several versions of timed feeders which mechanically portioned out the cat's food, allowing its owner to go away for the weekend; and a pet motel in Illinois that offered apartments, roomettes and imperial suites to guest cats at varied rates. California, always in the forefront of social fashion, could offer cats their own resort, department store, rest home, dating service, acting coaches, and cat psychics, and – for California's human citizens – a rent-a-cat agency.

A recent report in the **American weekly magazine**, the *National Enquirer*, suggests that in some respects the Californians are going too far. A company called Shelton Freeze Dry Taxidermy, in Orangevale, California, will freeze-dry your dead pet for you, in the same way that coffee is freeze-dried. The process takes from four to eight months and costs around $400 per pet, with its owner being given a guarantee that the pet will remain looking perfectly natural for at least 20 years. In the photographs accompanying the report Chang the cat and Gigi the poodle looked very lifelike as they relaxed in front of the television set, but . . .

OVERSEAS CATS

The Venetian cat, as a type, has its place in this list as the most famous of all city cats. Usually slim, elegant, not very large, and generally at the black-and-white, grey or tabby end of the feline colour spectrum, the Venetian cat makes an essential contribution to the unique magic atmosphere of a city where there is even a street named after cats: Salizzada delle Gatte. There were thought to be 40,000 cats in Venice before World War II and the numbers had not dropped by much when two English ladies, Miss Mabel Raymond-Hawkins and Mrs Helena Sanders, ran a highly public campaign on behalf of the supposedly starving and ill-treated cats of Venice in 1966. Their fund-raising activities in England and Venice drew in a famous novelist. Miss Nancy Mitford entered on the side of Venetians via the correspondence columns of the *Daily Telegraph* where she said that the ladies were misguided, Venice's cats were all right, and that the Venetians needed them as

essential rat catchers.

For some years now one of the sights on the regular tourist trips along the canals of **Amsterdam** has been a cat home. The intriguing sight is actually a barge, moored at Singel 40 in the centre of the city. Here, the barge's owner, Mrs van Weelde, has established a home for stray cats and, to judge by the number of cats to be seen relaxing on board, it is a pretty popular place with Amsterdam's homeless felines. The barge is open to visitors every afternoon between 1 and 2 – donations towards the cost of cat food welcome!

The word for 'cat' in other languages:

Bulgarian	kotki
Czechoslovakian	kŏcka
Danish and Dutch	kat
English	cat (Old English – cattle)
Finnish	kissa
French	chat
German	Katze
Greek	catta
Indian	billy
Irish	cāit
Italian	gatto
Japanese	neko
Maltese	qattus
Mexican	gato
Norwegian	katt
Polish	kot
Russian	koshka
Spanish and Portuguese	gato
Swedish	katt
Swiss	chaz
Turkish	tekir
Yugoslavian	macka

Caring societies

The relationship between people and cats has its dark side: thousands of domestic cats are abandoned every year and left to fend for themselves. It must be a plus for the people side of the relationship, however, that numerous organisations and charities have been set up to take care of animals in general, and cats in particular. Four in the UK are:

Cats Protection League
17 Kings Road, Horsham, W. Sussex RH13 5PP; tel. Horsham (0403) 65566.
A voluntary organisation with 140 groups and branches and 7 rescue centres throughout the UK. The League advocates the neutering of cats to prevent unwanted births, and can contribute towards the cost of veterinary fees for the operation in cases of hardship. In 1987 the League helped over 87,000 cats and kittens finding homes for about 47,000 stray and abandoned cats.

Feline Advisory Bureau
6 Woodthorpe Road, London SW15 6UQ; tel. 01 789 9553.
Another voluntary organisation, the Bureau offers a free and confidential advisory service on all aspects of cat care and ownership and is particularly good about advising on disease prevention and cure. Its inspection and approval scheme for boarding catteries is available to cat owners. The Bureau handles telephone queries on Tuesday, Wednesday and Thursday afternoons from 2 to 6.

People's Dispensary for Sick Animals (PDSA)
PDSA House, South Street, Dorking, Surrey RH4 2LB;

The Cats Protection League celebrated its silver jubilee in 1987. The picture shows Sylvia Davidson, a CPL helper, with some of her 30 foster cats.

tel. Dorking (0306) 888291
The PDSA is a registered charity, founded in 1917 to provide free veterinary treatment for animals whose owners could not afford private veterinary fees. Today it runs animal treatment centres and auxiliary centres through private vets throughout the country. At these centres, pet owners eligible for the PDSA's charitable service can have their pets treated free of charge. In 1987 the PDSA's centres treated 234,686 cats.

Established in 1917 to treat all animals, in 1987 the PDSA treated 234,686 cats.

Royal Society for the Prevention of Cruelty to Animals (RSPCA)
Headquarters, The Causeway, Horsham, W. Sussex; tel. Horsham (0403) 64181
The UK's major animal charity, the RSPCA cares for animals via a large countrywide network of branches. In 1987 it provided 194,132 treatments for animals, approximately a third of them cats. It found homes for 49,509 cats, but was forced to humanely destroy about 55,000.

CAT-SITTING REGISTER
Not a society – just Mrs Sybil Thompson of Great Missenden, Bucks, performing a much-needed service. She has compiled the UK's first list of cat sitters offering their services for emergencies, holidays, and similar situations.

Sleep is a favourite pastime of most cats. Pen and wash drawing by Giovanni Battista Tiepolo.

The Inimitable Cat

Cats are finding their way into our homes and hearts in increasing numbers. In Britain in the mid-1980s there were estimated to be 6.1 million house cats, compared with just 4 million in the mid-1970s. The 34 million pet cats in the United States today represent an increase of 55 per cent in just ten years.

However the cat still maintains an air of mystery which helps to perpetuate the many myths surrounding its remarkable agility and famed 'nine lives'. And it seems that the more we learn about our feline companions the more fascinating they become.

The physical aspect

The cat has an extra eyelid, the haw or nictitating membrane, which it can draw upwards across its eye from the inner corner to filter light. If the haw is raised over the cat's eye for any length of time, it can be an indication that the cat is ill.

Recent experiments have convinced scientists that, far from having only a monochrome view of the world, cats can distinguish between different colours. Whereas the human eye has three kinds of cone, absorbing red, green and blue light, the cat's eye has been found to contain cones sensitive to green and blue, though not to red. After long, patient training, cats have managed to distinguish the colour difference between red and blue objects and between these two colours and white, though it is probable that green, yellow and white look much the same to a cat, while red looks dark grey.

The average cat will have its eyes firmly closed for much of the time, especially as it gets older: observers have noted that the average cat sleeps 18 hours a day.

The cat's 30 teeth are specially adapted for stabbing, slicing and biting, and are so arranged that it can sever a rodent's spine with the precision of a surgeon.

The cat's saliva is thought to contain a deodorising, detergent-like substance which helps it to keep its fur clean.

The cat's tongue has a group of large papillae, pointing backwards and rough to the touch, on the upper surface. The cat uses them as its comb, for cleaning and grooming its fur.

The cat has a small pouch lined with receptor cells in the roof of its mouth, called the vomeronasal sac or Jacobson's organ. It is part of the cat's smelling mechanism and allows it to identify scents. That strange expression of distaste the cat may give, drawing its lips back from its teeth while raising its head, is called the 'flehmen' reaction and indicates that it is actually savouring some new smell that has wafted across its nostrils, passing it back to the Jacobson's organ.

Cats cannot see in the dark – or, at least, in total darkness. But the formation of their eyes means that they can see in much dimmer light than humans.

The familiar glow of the cat's eyes in the dark is caused by light which has passed through the eye and has not been absorbed by the retina. The light strikes a special layer of iridescent cells, the *tapetum lucidum* – also found in other nocturnal animals – creating the glow.

The cat's skeleton contains 230 bones, compared with 206 in man.

The cat's heart beats approximately 110–140 times a minute, which is about a third again as fast as the human heart.

A normal cat's fur contains three kinds of hair – guard hairs, bristle or awn hairs, and wool or down hairs. The first two are in the cat's top coat, where they act as protective covering, and the down hairs form the cat's insulating undercoat.

The cat has three sets of pressure-sensitive hairs, or vibrissae. The most obvious ones are the whiskers, extremely sensitive hairs growing in rows on the upper lip. Relaxed, the cat holds its whiskers sideways and back; when alert, its whiskers extend forward as the ca puffs out its whisker pads. The other vibrissae are the eyebrows and the long hairs on the underside of the front paws.

The cat's backbone, which contains five more bones than the human backbone, is uniquely flexible, which accounts for its legendary ability to land on its feet. Experiments with cats have shown that, dropped up-side down from a height of only 1 ft (30 cm), an alert cat can turn itself to land on all four paws in 1.8 seconds.

CATISTICS

The domestic cat is obviously not the largest of the felines, but neither is it the smallest, an honour which goes to the rusty-spotted cat (*Felis rubiginosa*) and the black-footed cat (*Felis nigripes*) which is smaller than *Felis rubiginosa* but generally weighs more. Just a fraction larger than either is the Kodkod, a wild cat found in Chile in the foothills of the Andes; its head and body together measure 16–19 in (41–48 cm), plus its tail, which is usually 9 in (23 cm) or less.

The average domestic cat weighs somewhere between 5–12 lb (2–5 kg), with the average female weight being rather less than that of the average male. The largest domestic cat, the American Ragdoll, can weigh three times the average. There have, of course, been many exceptions to the average.

BIG CATS

In the mid-1970s the slot in *The Guinness Book of Records* reserved for the world's heaviest domestic cat on record was filled by a ginger and white tom, called

Spice, from Ridgefield, Connecticut in the USA. Spice's top weight was 43 lb (19.54 kg); as with many very heavy cats, Spice's weight was largely due to a hypothyroid condition.

In 1977, the year that Spice died, the *Toronto Star* newspaper reported on Boots, a black-and-white alley cat, said to weigh a massive 53 lb (23.85 kg), the highest body weight ever attributed to a domestic cat, but the weight was not substantiated.

A bi-colour Ragdoll shows off his impressive 'vibrissae'.

Himmy, world heavyweight champion.

In 1989 *The Guinness Book of Records*' officially recognized world heavyweight record had reached 46 lb 15¼ oz (21.3 kg) in the shape of Himmy, a tom from Queensland in Australia. At this weight Himmy measured 15 in (38 cm) round the neck, 33 in (84 cm) round the middle and 38 in (97 cm) in length. He died in 1986 aged 10 years 4 months.

Even more rotund than Himmy, though weighing a few pounds less, was the 17-year-old, healthy neutered male, Tom, about which vet Mr George McKinney wrote to *The Guinness Book of Records* from Spencerport, New York in 1980. Tom's measurements were: neck 16½ in (41 cm), width, 36 in (91 cm), length 28 in (71 cm) (36 in to the tip of the tail), and he weighed 39 lb (17.6 kg).
In 1987 the British cat heavyweight record stood at 44½ lb (20 kg), which was the top weight of Poppa (born 1974), from Newport in Wales, before he was put on a diet. Since Poppa's daily food intake was reported as being one and a half tins of cat food, one tin of evaporated milk, two handfuls of cat biscuits, a selection of potatoes, carrots, cabbage and gravy and some homemade sponge cake, dieting was probably not a bad idea. Poppa died in June 1985, so the British heavyweight title is vacant at present.

LITTLE CATS

At the other end of the scale, where the smallest domestic cat is considered to be the Singapura, or 'Drain Cat' of Singapore, with an average male weight of 6 lb (2.7 kg) and a female weight of 4 lb (1.8 kg), there have also been smaller cats recorded.

In the late 1970s, there was Bumble Bee, for instance, a blue-grey tabby from Hassocks, in Sussex. At a year old, Bumble Bee weighed a touch over 3 lb (1.35 kg) and was 8 in (20 cm) high at the shoulder.

Even Bumble Bee seems quite large when compared with Britain's smallest recorded domestic cat, Pete, born in 1973. Pete never exceeded 2 lb (907 g) throughout his life.

In February 1984, Ebony-Eb-Honey Cat, a male Siamese/Manx cross from Boise, Idaho, USA, tipped the scales at only 1 lb 12 oz (79 g) when he was 23 months old.

A cat's age

Cats are generally considered to be young adults at five to six months old, reaching full body maturity at about one year.

The often-recounted way of comparing a cat's age with that of humans – multiplying the cat's years by seven – should not apply to older cats, say some experts. Once a cat is nearing feline old age, you should multiply its years by ten to arrive at a true comparison. If accurate, this would make the world's oldest known cats Methuselahs indeed.

Researchers have established, though with reservations, that male cats which have been castrated and spayed females generally live longer than intact cats, while intact females tend to live at least two years longer on average than intact males. It also seems that pure-bred cats live shorter lives on average than ordinary cats.

Although the average well-cared for, well-fed domestic cat may be expected to live for about 12 years, cats older than this are common and it is not unknown for cats to live for more than 25 years. Experts, backed by statistics, point out that greatly improved cat care, especially medical care, has increased the domestic cat's life expectancy by an average six to eight years in the past 30 years, putting them nearer a 16–20 years expectancy.

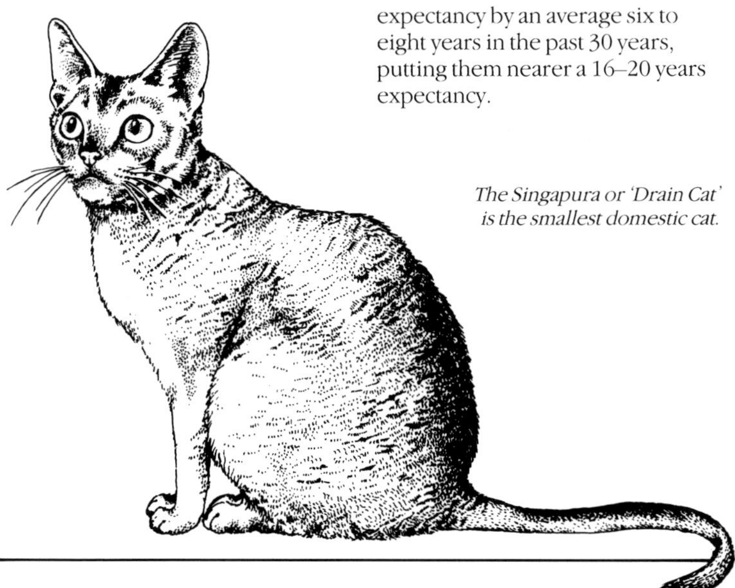

The Singapura or 'Drain Cat' is the smallest domestic cat.

Cats from Devon hold both the male and female cat longevity records. The world's oldest recorded cat, a tabby tom called Puss, died near Cullompton, the day after his 36th birthday in 1939. The world's oldest known female cat was Ma, from Drewsteighnton, who was 34 when she died in 1957.

The maternal instinct

Cats make good mothers, and not just of their own kittens. A queen will happily nurse the offspring of quite different species of animal immediately after giving birth to her own kittens; back in the 18th century, Gilbert White noted in *A Natural History of Selborne* local family pets who mothered a leveret and new-born squirrels. Scientists tell us that the reason for this is that the female cat is biologically programmed to respond to her kittens simply as small, warm, animate creatures requiring her attention. After some weeks, once her own kittens have turned into individuals, she will not accept other animals for nursing. Once her kittens are leaving her side for short periods to forage about for themselves, however, she may well nurse any kitten that comes back to her, even if it belongs to another mother cat in the same household.

The cat's gestation period averages 65 days, with her average size of litter, or kindle, being two to six young.

The largest cat litter on record contained 19 kittens, four of them stillborn, born after a 70-day gestation, to a 4-year-old brown Burmese, Tarawood Antigone, of Kingham in Oxfordshire in 1970. The 15 survivors, 14 of them male, all grew to healthy, larger-than-average adults.

The largest known litter in which all the kittens born survived, was the 14-strong kindle of a Persian called Bluebell, produced in Wellington, Cape Province, South Africa, in 1974.

Wild cats normally have only one

litter a year, but domestic cats, if well cared-for and well-nourished, can produce two or three litters a year. In her reproductive life, a female cat may well produce more than 100 offspring.

A tabby called Dusty, from Bonham, Texas, USA, did much better than this. She produced 420 kittens, the last one of which was born when she was 18 years old in 1952.

The British prolific-mother record has been held since 1933 by another tabby, this one called Tippy, from Kingston-upon-Hull, Humberside, who produced her 343rd kitten when she was 21.

The average healthy queen can produce kittens until she is 15–18 years old, but here again, there have been exceptions even older than Tippy. One such was black-and-white Tish, of Maltby in Yorkshire. She was 25 when she produced her 100th and 101st kittens in 1958.

There is also a cat known to have produced her *first* kitten at an even greater age. Tortoiseshell Smitty

Koko and her tiny feline friend, Lips-Lipstick.

had retired in 1953 aged 28 from a lifetime spent rat catching when the maternal instinct took over and she allowed herself to be seduced, producing one perfectly healthy kitten.

A cat who achieved some fame as a foster mother was Beauty, the found-in-a-cat-home pet of English naturalist Dr John Paling. Dr Paling was making a film study of the habits of squirrels in 1978 and gave Beauty an orphaned squirrel to nurse. Beauty and her fine, healthy 'squitten' featured in Dr Paling's television film and in his subsequent book, *Squirrel on My Shoulder*.

In 1986 the life of Lucky, a day-old Jack Russell which was left to die on a rubbish dump at Rotherham in South Yorkshire, was saved when he was mothered in kennels by Tibby, a cat with kittens of her own.

Sometimes it is other animals who need kittens to satisfy their own maternal instincts. Koko, a female gorilla with a 500-word vocabulary, was bereft when the kitten she had looked after at the Gorilla Foundation in California was killed by a car in 1985. The Foundation's staff gave Koko a tiny ginger Manx kitten, which he named Lips-Lipstick, as a replacement. Koko was delighted. 'My cat good', she signalled to her keepers as she hugged and caressed the kitten.

Body language

Konrad Lorenz wrote that 'few animals display their mood via facial expressions as distinctly as the cat'. Their body gestures, too, can speak volumes – as much as their voices. Some signals to watch out for:

If the cat flattens its *ears*, it is **annoyed** or **frightened**. Twitching them back and forth quickly usually indicates anxiety.

Another sign of **worry** or **anxiety** are two quick flicks of the *tongue* round the lips, especially if the cat is also watching something closely.

The cat's *tail* offers as clear a series of messages as a Navy signaller's flags. When a male cat holds its tail bent forward over its head it is signalling that it is the **top cat** of the area. When it lashes it to and fro, it is making a clear sign of **anger**. **Excited**, and the tip of its tail quivers. A **contented** cat may wave its tail quietly from side to side like a lady's fan. A cat may be to all appearances asleep, but if its tail moves about, that is a signal that it is still **alert** and **ready to spring into action**. Cats will also use their tail as a **greeting** signal, giving it a stiff, quick flick upwards, a gesture it may use both for people and for other cats.

A **greeting** gesture generally reserved for people is that quick *hop* a cat will often perform, lifting both its front paws off the ground together and putting them down again. It may rub itself against your legs too, either as it is hopping or immediately afterwards.

A rarer form of **greeting**, and one that indicates complete trust in you, involves the cat rolling on to its back to display its *stomach*. Sometimes, a cat will ask for a caress by flopping down on its side.

The signals given by a cat **about to attack** are unmistakable: the back held high, tail straight up, ears flattened, the irises of the eye dilated and the teeth showing in a ferocious snarl all add up to a very dangerous animal indeed.

A cat expresses **fright** in every line of its body; crouched low, its body is as flattened to the ground as possible, its fur stands up all over its body, and its eyes dilate.

A cat rubbing its head or the side of its chin against objects is very likely **marking out its territory**, for the cat uses scent glands to signal to other cats that certain places are its preserve. The glands, on the forehead and round the mouth and chin, produce chemicals called pheromones which the cat transfers to objects by rubbing.

Cats, especially un-neutered males, also **mark their territory** by spraying with urine which also contains pheromones. Other cats pick up the scent and its unmistakable message instantly. Some experts think that cats can also judge how long ago the scent was laid and, therefore, how much notice they need take of it.

Cat chat

The vocal language of cats is extensive. Most cat owners will recognise these vocalisations: the chirrups and squeaks of kittens; the noises and calls of a mother cat disciplining her young; the cat's demanding meow when it is trying to attract your attention; the special call of a female in season and the catterwauling of an aggressive tom; or all the growls, hisses, spittings and screams that accompany cat fights. Although it is now more than 40 years since the American scientist, Dr Mildred Moelk, published her extremely detailed scientific survey of the vocal language of the cat, the mechanisms of the cat's many noises, and of the cat's distinctive purr, are still not fully understood.

Dr Moelk divided the cat's speech into three basic sound groups: **murmurs**, made with the mouth closed; **calls**, during which the cat's mouth starts off open then slowly closes; and **cries**, in which the mouth is held rigidly open throughout.

The cat's **purr** comes from two membranous folds, called the false vocal cords, situated in the cat's larynx behind the vocal cords. The cat's typical smooth purr usually indicates contentment; a shorter, purr-like noise usually seems like a comment on something; while a deep purr may indicate that the cat is in pain or distress.

Feline fare

Weight for weight, cats eat half as much again in terms of the calories they consume as do humans, and – again weight for weight – they also eat much bigger amounts than we do. The average cat consumes about 127,750 calories a year, eating nearly 28 times its weight in food in a year to obtain those calories, and it tops up with the same amount again in liquids.

Much of the food served to cats in the Western world, especially in Western Europe and North America, comes out of the tins, packets and boxes of pet-food manufacturers. In Britain, 90 per cent of cat owners give their pets canned food at least once a week.

In 1985, Britain's 6.1 million cats consumed 397,000 tonnes of canned food and 26,000 tonnes of other cat foods, including biscuits, at a total retail selling price of £333 million. Meanwhile, across the Atlantic in the United States, which first gave the world tinned pet foods before World War II, about 34 million cats (1982 estimate) were chewing their way through more than a million tons of cat food, to a total retail value of $1.4 billion.

Cats also appreciate more exotic fare. Many cat owners will recognize their own cats' tastes among the list of her Birman's eating fads which Mrs Lorraine Ford sent to *Cat World* magazine in 1985: grapes (pips neatly spat out in a pile), garlic cheese, chilli con carne, plain pasta (fresh, for preference), baked beans, corn kernels, mashed potato, hard-boiled eggs, yoghurt with Greek honey, cake and ice lollies. Another writer to the same magazine said his Devon Rex would sell his soul for a spear of asparagus!

The cat remains a natural carnivore, unlike the dog who, along with humans, is an omnivore and could even survive on a vegetarian diet provided it was a sensible one. The cat's own body metabolism cannot make certain essential chemicals, so it must obtain these from the bodies of other animals. The cat also needs a large daily intake of protein – twice that of dogs – and it can obtain the right kind of protein in sufficiently large quantities only from animal products such as fish, meat, offal, milk and eggs. Fortunately, our pampered, town-bred moggy's basic food needs are well understood by scientists, so that the contents of a good quality tin of cat food is just about the best balanced meal he could get.

The raw materials that go into cat foods are generally ones that are unsuitable for, or surplus to, human consumption. In the UK in 1985, pet-food manufacturers used 391,000 tonnes of meat and meat by-products (which must, by law, be sterilised before they go into the chain of distribution); 55,000

A cat's love of fish will usually overcome its hatred of water. Watercolour by Kalighat c. *1890.*

tonnes of fish; and 144,000 tonnes of cereals.

A chemical that it has been suggested manufacturers should add to canned cat food is tourine. It was recently discovered that without this essential chemical in their diet, which, in the wild, cats obtain through the meat of their prey, cats may go blind. In Britain in 1982 the Animal Health Trust established how much tourine should go into tinned cat food.

Even well-fed cats will eat grass. It is thought that grass provides cats with necessary traces of folic acid and aids their digestive processes. Cocks Foot grass is particularly favoured by discerning cats. It is a natural emetic, relieving the stomach of sourness, and it helps cats vomit fur balls.

People who remark that their cat is 'crazy about' toy catnip mice may be nearer the literal truth than they know. Catnip, *Nepata cataria*, exudes a scent that many cats find highly intoxicating, with about 50 per cent of the world's feline population showing some response to it. In things like catnip mice and scratching posts, the scent comes from the essential oil of the plant, nepetalactone, which is extracted from it and, diluted, is used to attract and trap wild cats. It is thought that the capacity to detect nepetalactone is inherited; cats that do respond to it often fall into a trance-like state which may last for ten minutes or more. Other aromatic plants to which cats seem strongly attracted include valerian (a kind of heliotrope) and 'cat thyme' (*Teucrium manum*).

The 18th-century naturalist **Gilbert White** thought the cat's strong liking for fish was against nature. 'There is a propensity belonging to common house cats that is very remarkable,' he noted in *A Natural History of Selborne*; 'I mean their violent fondness of fish, which appears to be their most favourite food; and yet nature, in this instance, seems to have planted in them an appetite that, unassisted, they know not how to gratify; for of all quadrupeds, cats are the least disposed towards water; and will not, when they can avoid it, deign to wet a foot, much less to plunge into that element.'

Gilbert White was talking about that invention of the statistician, the 'average cat'. On the whole, he was right about the cat's dislike of water, but there have been numerous instances recorded of domestic cats who have been expert at catching fish, and even of cats who liked drinking with their paws. There was 19-year-old Jerry, for instance, who was a star attraction in the bar of the Town of Ramsgate at Wapping Old Stairs in the early 1960s. The stylish way he drank beer from a glass with his paw got him into the national newspapers.

Scientists say that cats show no particular response to sweet tastes, but are very sensitive to water tastes. Many will ignore clean bowls of fresh water and lap instead from swimming pools, stagnant ponds or puddles. Often, they will lap up puddles of such dangerous liquids as car anti-freeze which requires immediate veterinary treatment.

Endurance records

The cat's splendid, strongly

muscled physique is what gets it out of trouble as much as its fabled 'nine lives', though there is no denying that cats seem able to survive incidents and accidents that other beings would not.

Experts say that few cats would survive a fall of more than 60 feet or so, but there have been incidents of cats surviving falls of much greater distances than that. *The Guinness Book of Pet Records'* 'greatest authenticated fall' record is held by a female black-and-white cat called **Patricia**. The cat was a year old and pregnant when she was thrown off St John's Bridge in Portland, Oregon, USA, in March 1981, landing in the cold waters of the Willamett River 205 ft (62 m) below. She was rescued by two fishermen and, although she aborted her kittens and had to have an operation, she recovered.

On dry land the fall-and-survive record stands at 200 ft (61 m), which was the distance two-year-old ginger and white tom, **Gros Minou**, fell from the balcony of his owner's 20th-floor apartment in Outrement, Quebec State, Canada in 1973. Gros Minou landed in a flower bed and sustained an undisplaced fracture of the pelvis. Within a week he was crawling about, albeit slowly, again.

Even animals as sure-footed as the cat can miss their step, as a female cat called **Tabby** did in Sydney, Australia. She slid off a roof and dropped 50 ft (15 m) down a drainpipe, where she stuck fast. The Sydney police got her out, ruffled but all right, by cutting a hole in the drainpipe with a tin opener and a panel cutter.

Domestic curiosity nearly killed two cats in Britain in the first month of 1986. There was **Victa**, who got shut in a refrigerator for 12 hours. A vet was called, who pronounced her dead when he was apparently unable to resusitate her. Then, Victa suddenly stood up and walked. Her owner, a young student, said it was a miracle – literally. She had prayed to St Francis of Assisi for Victa, and her prayer had been heard.

Then there was 5-month-old **Harvey**, a smoky Persian. His adventure in his owner's washing machine, when he went through ten minutes of the automatic wash cycle before he was spotted amongst the family laundry and rescued, made BBC television's main news broadcast of the day. Rinsed and dried out under a hairdryer, and apparently none the worse for it all, Harvey was shown still sitting in front of the washing machine watching, with 'satiable curtiosity', the clothes going round.

English cat owner **Mrs Christine Webb** was horrified when she saw her 14-year-old pet cat swallow a needle and thread. After some days the cat, while cleaning herself, pulled out the thread, still attached to the needle. When Mrs Webb told

The Guinness Book of Records of the incident her cat had reached the great age of 21.

A ginger tom called **Timmy**, looking for a quiet place for a rest while out walking in Southampton, squeezed through a 4 in (10 cm) hole in a wall which was being rebuilt. As he snoozed, workmen came along and completed the wall. Timmy was bricked up for 24 days before his mewings were heard and the police and fire brigade rescued him, little the worse for his entombment.

An even more striking feat of endurance was that of a six-year-old cat, **Peter**, who was trapped below decks when the motor vessel, *Tjoba*, overturned and sank after a collision on the River Rhine. It was eight days before the boat was pulled back to the surface and Peter was discovered alive in the master's cabin, where he had survived in an air pocket.

Long air journeys by cats have included those of **Hamlet** in 1984 and **Felix** in 1988. Hamlet was an official passenger on a British Air Boeing 727 flight from Toronto to London when he escaped from his cage. He took in Australia, Kuwait, Singapore and Jamaica on his 60,000-mile (96,000 km), six-week trip before cargo workers caught up with him. **Felix** climbed out of her travelling box *en route* from Frankfurt to Los Angeles and was found 29 days later, by which time she had visited three continents and flown 180,000 miles (288,000 km). Both cats are believed to have survived by sipping condensation droplets in the cargo holds.

Another near six-week journey survived was the 41-day sea voyage of a cat nailed up in a crate with a diesel engine shipped from the USA to Cairo in Egypt. The cat survived by licking engine oil and even managed to produce a litter of **four kittens** on her journey.

TRAVELLIN' CATS

The famed ability of cats to get many hundreds of miles across country to return home or to link up again with former owners is seen by some experts as a sign that extra-sensory perception plus some kind of navigational instinct (also known in birds, for instance) are inherent in the cat's make-up. They accept that the cat's ability to return to an old home after being taken away from it may have a lot to do with its strong territorial instinct, but how to explain a cat's turning up at an owner's new home, which the cat has never been to, and which is sometimes hundreds of miles from the old home? Here are some well-founded and widely reported incidents to ponder.

A two-year-old part-Persian, **Sugar**, was left behind with a neighbour in her home town of Anderson,

California, when her family moved 1,500 miles (2,414 km) across the United States to Gage in Oklahoma. Her owners thought that this was the kindest thing to do with Sugar since she had a congenitally deformed hip and did not like car travel. Two weeks after her owners' departure, Sugar also disappeared. Fourteen months after that she turned up in Gage on her old owners' doorstep.

Sugar's average speed of 100 miles (161 km) a month puts her in the supercat category. Four-year-old **Chat Beau**, for instance, another American long-distance record-holder, was rather slower; it took him four months to do the near-300 miles (483 km) between his old home in Lafayette, Louisiana and his owners' new home in Texarkana, Texas, and two-year old **Pooh** spent four months covering the 200 miles (322 km) between his owners' old home in Newnan, Georgia and their new one in Wellford, South Carolina. A three-year-old Persian called **Smoky** sounds as if he strolled along admiring the view, since he took 12 months to cover the 417 miles (671 km) between his owners' former home in Tulsa, Oklahoma and their new place in Memphis, Tennessee.

Wasting no time at all was a cat called **Rusty**, whose American all-time speed record, set in 1949, has not yet been equalled. It is assumed that Rusty hitched himself lifts on trucks, cars and trains because he caught up with his owners in Chicago, Illinois, just 83 days after setting out from Boston, Massachusetts, 950 miles (1529 km) away.

The British record for this sort of thing is much shorter, though since Britain is a comparatively small country, this is not surprising. The record is held by a three-year-old tabby called **McCavity** who took only three weeks to cover the 500 miles (805 km) from his new home in Cumbernauld back south to Truro in Cornwall.

And for sheer determination to hang on rather than get left behind, spare a thought for young **Tiger**, who climbed on to the roof-rack of the family car in the summer of 1985, and stayed there, along with a couple of bikes and a tent, for more than 100 miles from North Wales to a service area on the M6 motorway, where he was spotted and taken into the car.

MASTER MOUSERS

Some cats have set records simply by continuing to do what they are good at on a grand scale. Take **Towser**, the world's champion mouser. Towser was born in the still house of Scotland's oldest working distillery, the Glenturret Distillery near Crieff, Perthshire, on 21 April 1963. Up to June 1986, she was catching an average three mice a day, and rather more in the spring, giving her a grand total of more than 25,000 mice.

The 'greatest mouser on record' title was held by a tabby called **Mickey** who, in 23 years with the firm of Shepherd and Sons Ltd of Burscough, Lancashire, caught 22,000 mice. Mickey died in 1968.

The 'greatest ratter on record' was another tabby, this time a female called **Minnie** who in the six years from 1927 to 1933 caught 12,480 rats in the White City Stadium in London.

Towser – Master Mouser, 1963–1987.

Famous cats

Cats well-known mainly because they have belonged to famous people are listed elsewhere in this book. Here are some cats famous in their own right.

Two cats have places in the history of the **Tower of London**. We know the names of neither, though we do know what one of them looked like. This was the cat belonging to Henry Wriothesley, 3rd Earl of Southampton and one-

time patron of William Shakespeare. Southampton unwisely became involved in the Earl of Essex's rebellion in 1601 and was thrown into the Tower. There, his cat sought him out, finding his way to his master down a chimney, and remained with him during his captivity. Southampton had his portrait painted in prison, and included his cat, a solemnly self-possessed black-and-white puss with large amber eyes.

The Tower's other famous cat was the one which brought pigeons as food to its owner, Sir Henry Wyat, during his imprisonment in the Tower. Sir Henry had been Keeper of the Jewels to both Henry VII and Henry VIII, but was imprisoned when he lost the favour of the latter. Sir Henry survived because of his beloved cat's initiative and because he had a jailer sympathetic enough to cook the pigeons!

The Dicken Medal – the 'Animals' VC' – was instituted by Mrs Maria Dicken, founder of the People's Dispensary for Sick Animals, for animals displaying conspicuous gallantry and devotion to duty associated with the Armed Forces during World War II and its aftermath. The only cat to win the medal was **Simon**, the black-and-white cat, born in Hong Kong, who served on board HMS *Amethyst* during the Yangtse Incident in 1949 and was in the Commander's cabin when the shell which wounded him – and killed Lt. Cdr. I.R. Griffiths – exploded. Simon's medal citation reads: 'Served on HMS Amethyst during the Yangtse Incident, disposing of many rats though wounded by shell blast. Throughout the incident his behaviour was of the highest order, although the blast was capable of making a hole over a foot in diameter in a steel plate.' Simon was brought back to England where he died later in 1949. He was buried in the PDSA's pet's cemetery at Ilford in Essex and a special tombstone was carved for him by Elizabeth Munz in Corfe. *Note:* The Royal Navy banned cats from its ships in 1975, feeling that the danger of importing rabies into Britain outweighed their usefulness on modern ships, so there will be no more heroes like Simon for us to honour.

A cat well-known to visitors to the British Museum early this century was **Mike**, who helped keep the Museum's main gate in Great Russell Street for 20 years. The eminent Egyptologist and Keeper of Egyptian and Assyrian Antiquities at the Museum, Sir Ernest Wallis Budge, contributed sixpence a week to the cat's upkeep, and was one of only two people Mike would allow to pet him (the other was the official gatekeeper). After Mike's death in 1929, Sir Ernest wrote and published a solemn 16-page monograph extolling the virtues of 'Mike the cat who assisted in Keeping the Main Gate of the British Museum from February 1909 to January 1929'.

Smudge, successful rodent operative at Glasgow's People's Palace since 1980 and the only female (and, at 12 years old, the youngest) member of Branch 29 of the General, Municipal, Boilermakers and Allied Trades Union, has been immortalised in porcelain. Modelled by Scottish artist Margery Clinton, Smudge's 'replicat' was first sold in 1986 in a

Smudge and his 'replicats'.

limited edition of 50 life-size models, proceeds to go to the People's Palace. These sold out so fast that Mrs Clinton was commissioned to make another, smaller version, so now a great many more visitors to the People's Palace may have a copy of the first 'Glasgow wally (ceramic) cat' to be produced this century.

Hamlet was resident cat at the Algonquin Hotel in New York for 12 years until his death, aged about 15, in 1982. Famous simply for being famous, Hamlet met most of the great names who stayed at the Algonquin, many of whom found that it was good publicity to be photographed with him. A book about Hamlet was called *Algonquin Cat* and was a well-illustrated look at the cat's life in the great hotel. Hamlet has had two successors, and Hamlet III is the latest Algonquin *chat d'hotel*.

Another cat famous in his lifetime for being famous was **Nini** the Frari cat, who lived in a coffee shop near the Frari church in Venice in the 1890s. If Nini is not forgotten today it is because Jan Morris has included the story of the splendid white tom in her writings about Venice, most recently in *A Venetian Bestiary* (Thames and Hudson, 1982). Nini, carefully exploited by the café owner, became the smart thing for visitors to call upon in the city. Among these, Jan Morris tells us, 'were Pope Leo XIII, the Czar Alexander III, the King and Queen of Italy, Prince Paul Metternich, the Negus Menelik Salamen and Verdi, who scribbled a few notes from Act III of *La Traviata* in Nini's visitors' book'. Nini died in 1894.

In 1967 a splendidly large and handsome white Persian cat, **Grand Champion Coylum Marcus**, was appointed the United States White Persian Society's first ambassador to Britain. Guest of honour at cat shows all over Britain, Coylum Marcus travelled in style enthroned on a gold pneumatic cushion in a travelling pavilion draped with silver lamé curtains and drapes fringed in blue and gold. The cat was British born and bred, but was appointed to his high diplomatic office on account of his superb show record.

A cat who worked with four British prime ministers was **Wilberforce**, official cat at Number 10 Downing Street during the occupancies of **Edward Heath**, **Harold Wilson**, **James Callaghan** and **Margaret Thatcher**. Wilberforce, who was obtained from the RSPCA attended Cabinet meetings, but kept his thoughts on them to himself. He retired in 1987 after 18 year's service and died in 1988.

Tiddles, a massive 32 lb (14.5 kg) tabby, was one of the most famous railway cats in Britain in the 1970s. He lived at Paddington Station in London, making his base the ladies cloakroom on Platform 1, into which he had crept as a six-week-old kitten in 1970s, for 13 years. Kept well supplied with best quality food by admiring travellers, Tiddles lived to celebrate royal weddings, birthdays and similar events in flag-bedecked style before dying in 1983.

Another well-known railway moggie was **Black Sam**, who lived a few stops along the Underground lines from Tiddles at Kings Cross station. Black Sam lived in his own home, provided by a thoughtful and caring commuter, on Platform 10 for more than 10 years.

In 1986 the British news media took to their hearts a 15-month-old black cat called **Snowy**, the station cat at Bristol's busy Temple Meads railway station. Railway staff worried about Snowy's all-too-frequent away days, when he would go off the rails, so to speak, in pursuit of lady cats, hopping on board trains bound for all parts of the country. They decided Snowy would have to be neutered to stop his wanderings and launched an appeal to cover the vet's costs. Then a local vet stepped in, offering to perform the operation for free. Snowy, safely convalescent, was showered with gifts from rail passengers.

LAST IN LINE

Peta was the last of a long line of official cats at the Home Office, stretching back to 1883. Until Peta, a female black Manx, was given to the then Home Secretary, Sir Henry Brooke, by the Isle of Man government in 1964, the Home Office cat had always been a black male, and was always called Peter. Peta, on five shillings a day meal allowance from public funds, fulfilled her role with grace and dignity until she was retired in 1974.

Another 'last' cat was **Charlie**, the last official cat at the Royal Navy shore base at Chatham, which was closed in 1982. Charlie was only a year old when he was run over in November 1981, but he had a pay book and a service number – C1111115 – and so, as a member of Her Majesty's armed forces, was given a funeral with full naval honours, including the Last Post, a flower-bedecked coffin with bearers in uniform, and the base flag at half-mast.

And, finally, a brief tribute to **Blackie**, the last cat at the Post Office's London Headquarters building, though not, it is hoped,

the last in a proud line of Post Office cats stretching back to 1868 and taking in post offices, sorting office and storerooms all over the country. Blackie inherited his job as cat-in-charge at the Post Office Headquarters from his mother in 1972, a job which she had obtained simply by walking in off the street in 1971, pregnant. Thus Blackie was born in the PO and there he stayed, proving an efficient mouser, until his death in June 1984. In his time, he saw his pay rise from £1 to £2 a week and, a photogenic cat, appeared on television.

The Pedigree Cat

Cats began to become 'pedigree' animals rather than simple domestic pets and mousers from the latter part of the 19th century, when people started taking an interest in the origins and different physical characteristics of cats. The Russian (or Archangel) cat, the Angora and, later, the Persian, had been coming into Europe in increasing numbers from the 16th century. From the mid-19th century they were joined in Britain by such exotic imports as the Abyssinian, brought to England by Mrs Burrett Lennard, wife of an officer serving with Lord Napier's military expedition to Abyssinia in the 1860s, and the Siamese, which was first shown to the public at a Crystal Palace cat show in 1886, having been brought out of Siam, where they had hitherto been jealously guarded, by Lady Dorothy Nevill, wife of the British Consul General.

The pedigree shapes Pedigree cats come in two basic shapes: a 'cobby' shape, with a round head, large in relation to the body, full round eyes and a short, thick body on sturdy legs; and a more lean and svelte shape, typified by the Siamese and other Orientals, in which the head is long and wedge-shaped, the eyes almond-shaped, the body and limbs elegant and the tail long and thin.

The pedigree groupings
Pedigree cats may be divided into six groupings:
Long-hairs or Persians; Short-hairs, including British, American, European and Domestic groups; Exotics (Persians crossed with short-hairs); Orientals (Siamese and Siamese-derived breeds); Semi-long-hairs (Oriental conformation with long, silky coats); and Foreign short-hairs.

Pedigree cat numbers Only a small percentage of Britain's cats are registered with the GCCF as pedigree animals; in 1985 new registrations on the four main registers – Long-hair, Short-hair, Siamese and Balinese – totalled 24,927. In the United States there are nearly 50,000 pedigree cats on the lists of the country's nine registry groups, which leaves the vast majority of America's 34 million-plus cats to be called simply moggs or alley-cats.

Registration requirements
These differ from one registering body to another. The cat must have a known, recorded ancestry going back several generations (usually five), it must be of an established breed, with its breeding

Shirar Snow Chieftain – now a Grand Champion Persian.

conforming to set rules and within recognized varieties.

The recognized British breeds

Breeds and varieties recognized by the Governing Council of the Cat Fancy (GCCF) in Britain at the beginning of 1987 were:

LONG-HAIR REGISTER

Persian Type Long-hairs
These are beautiful cats with short, stocky bodies, thick long fur and broad heads with a short broad nose, large eyes, small tufted ears and full, round cheeks.
Varieties Black, Blue-eyed white, Orange-eyed white, Odd-eyed white, Blue, Red Self, Cream, Smoke (Black), Blue smoke, Chocolate smoke, Lilac smoke, Silver Tabby (Black Silver), Brown Tabby (Black) Blue Tabby, Chocolate Tabby, Lilac Tabby, Red Tabby, Chinchilla, Tortoiseshell (Black), Chocolate Tortie, Lilac Tortie, Tortie and White (Black), Blue Tortie and White, Chocolate Tortie and White, Lilac Tortie and White, Black and White Bi-colour, Blue and White Bi-colour, Chocolate and White Bi-colour, Lilac and White Bi-colour, Red and

Van Guzelli Iskenderun, one of the first Turkish Vans to be imported into England, and her kitten, Van Kehribar.

White Bi-colour, Cream and White Bi-colour, Blue-Cream.

Persians (also called Himalayan Cats). This cat has full Persian characteristics plus the distinctive colour pattern of the Siamese and its blue eyes.

Colourpoint Seal Point, Blue Point, Chocolate Point, Lilac Point, Red Point, Seal Tortie Point, Cream Point, Blue-Cream Point, Chocolate Tortie Point, Lilac-Cream Point, Seal Tabby Point, Blue Tabby Point, Chocolate Tabby Point, Lilac Tabby Point, Red Tabby Point, Seal Tortie Tabby Point, Cream Tabby Point, Blue-Cream Tabby Point, Chocolate Tortie Tabby Point, Lilac-Cream Tabby Point.

Cameo and other varieties Chocolate Cameo, Lilac Cameo, Red Shell Cameo, Red Shaded Cameo, Red Smoke Cameo, Tortie Cameo (Black/Red), Cream Shell Cameo, Cream Shaded Cameo, Cream Smoke Cameo, Blue-Cream Cameo, Pewter, Golden Persian, Shaded Silver.

Birmans

Like the short-haired Burmese, this cat originated in Burma, but is otherwise quite different. Supposedly the sacred cat of the Temple of Lao Tsun, the Birman made a brief appearance in the west after World War I, and its breeding was revived in the 1960s.

Colourpoints The first ten in the Persian-type Colourpoints list are the recognised colourpoints for Birmans.

Tabby Point Birmans are still awaiting recognition by the GCCF and will follow the Long-hair Colourpoint numbering 11 to 20, i.e. Seal Tabby Point — Lilac-Cream Tabby Point (above).

Turkish

This is the Turkish 'Van' Cat, the cat which loves swimming. Two English cat breeders, Laura

Van Cats were discovered near Lake Van in Turkey and enjoy a swim.

Lushington and Sonia Halliday, found it near Lake Van in Turkey in 1955 and brought a pair back to England, where the breed was formally recognised in 1969. The Turkish is a chalk white cat with auburn marking on the face and auburn tails ringed with a darker auburn, pale amber eyes, pale pink nose and rims to the eyes.

SHORT-HAIR REGISTER

British Short-hairs

Varieties Blue-eyed White; Orange-eyed White; Odd-eyed White; Black; Chocolate; Lilac; Red Self; Blue; Cream; Silver Tabby (Black); Red Tabby; Brown Tabby (Black); Blue Tabby; Tortoiseshell (Black); Chocolate Tortie; Lilac-Cream Tortie; Tortie and White (Black); Blue Tortie and White; Blue-Cream; Spotted (Black) and a range of Blue, Chocolate, Lilac, Red and Cream Spotted; Silver Spotted and a range of Blue, Chocolate, Lilac, Red and Cream Silver Spotted; Black and White Bi-colour and a range of Blue and White,

Close-up of a British Blue, considered by many to be the epitome of the British Short-hairs.

Chocolate and White, Lilac and White, Red and White and Cream and White Bi-colours; Black Smoke and a range of Blue, Chocolate, Lilac, Red, Brown Tortie, Cream, Blue Tortie, Chocolate Tortie and Lilac Tortie Smokes; Black Tipped and a range of Blue, Chocolate, Lilac, Red, Brown Tortie, Cream, Blue Tortie, Chocolate Tortie and Lilac Tortie Tipped; and Colourpointed, the range of which is the same as the Long-hair Colourpoints (above).

Manx
This is the truly tailless cat said to have reached the Isle of Man from a Spanish Armada ship whose captain had probably picked the cat up in the Middle East. The cat has a rounded-off rump with a hollow where in other cats the tail would normally begin. Contrary to all the legends (see page 66), the taillessness is a genetic mutation.
Varieties Blue-eyed White; Orange-eyed White; Odd-eyed White; Green-eyed White; Black; Chocolate; Red Self; Blue; Cream; Silver Tabby and a range of Blue, Chocolate, Lilac, Red, Brown Tortie, Cream, Blue, Chocolate Tortie and Lilac Tortie, Silver Tabbies; Red Tabby; Brown Tabby; Tortie; Chocolate Tortie; Lilac Tortie; Tortie and White; Blue Tortie and White; Chocolate Tortie and White; Lilac Tortie and White; Blue-Cream; Spotted Manx and the same range of colours as the Silver Tabby; Silver Spotted and the same range of colours as the Silver Tabby; Black and White Bi-colour, and the same range of colours as the Silver Tabby; Black Smoke and White, and the same range of colours as the Silver Tabby; Brown Tabby and White, and the same

The true Manx has no tail at all, however some litters will produce a kitten with a short tail called a Stumpy.

range of colours as the Silver Tabby; Silver Tabby and White, and the same range of colours as the Silver Tabby; Smoke Manx, and the same range of colours as the Silver Tabby; Tipped Manx, and the same range of colours as the Silver Tabby; Stumpy Manx, a Manx with a short tail, in the complete colour range above; Tailed Manx, also in the complete colour range above.

FOREIGN SHORT-HAIRS

Abyssinian
Called the 'Ruddy' in the US, this is a modern version of the Egyptian Abyssinian brought to Europe in the 1860s. The cat has the 'agouti' coat pattern more usually found in wild cats, and has a form very like cats in ancient Egyptian paintings and sculptures.
Varieties Usual (Black), Sorrel, Chocolate, Blue, Lilac (Chocolate dilute), Fawn (Sorrel dilute), Red (sex-linked Red), Cream (sex-linked Cream), Tortie (Usual-Black), Sorrel Tortie, Chocolate Tortie, Blue Tortie, Lilac Tortie, Fawn Tortie, Silver (Usual-Black) Sorrel Silver, Chocolate Silver, Blue Silver, Lilac Silver, Fawn Silver, Red Silver (sex-linked Red), Cream Silver (sex-linked Cream), Tortie Silver (Usual-Black), Sorrel Tortie Silver, Chocolate Tortie Silver, Blue Tortie Silver, Lilac Tortie Silver, Fawn Tortie Silver.

Somali (long-haired)
This is a relatively new variety of cat, the result of mating the Abyssinian with a British long-hair, and has the typical Abyssinian physique.
Varieties Usual (Black), and the same colour range as the

Young Abyssinian sorrel.

Somali – a relatively new variety of cat.

Abyssinian, above; short-haired progeny of a mating with at least one Somali parent (Somali variant); the Sorrel Somali has been given provisional recognition by the GCCF.

Russian

This graceful cat is descended from the 'Archangel' cats so-called because sailors from Elizabethan times on brought them home from the north Russian port called Archangel.

Varieties Russian Blue, White Russian (green-eyed), Black Russian.

Korat

This cat from Thailand (Siam) was

The exotic and beautiful Korat is considered a 'good luck' cat.

known for centuries in its native land as *Si-Sawat*, a name which associated it with the bringing of good luck. A pair of these sturdy and muscular cats with startling green-gold eyes were first taken to North America in 1959 and the breed developed there. They received champion status recognition in Britain in 1984.

Cornish Rex
This cat first turned up as a mutation in a litter of otherwise normal kittens in Cornwall in 1950. It had a curly coat consisting almost entirely of down hairs, with no guard hairs. The first Cornish Rex was called Kallibunker and his son, Poldhu, carried on the line, with Poldhu's sister, Lamorna Cove, being exported to America to begin the line there.
Varieties Cornish Rex, and a range of colours following those listed for the Manx, above.

Devon Rex
Another curly-coated cat, though genetically quite distinct from the Cornish Rex, this cat first appeared in Devon in 1960. Its head, with its large, bat-wing-like ears and delicate, large-eyed face is quite different from that of the Cornish Rex.
Varieties Devon Rex and a range of colours following those listed for the Manx, above; and Cinnamon; Caramel; Cinnamon Tortie; Caramel Tortie; Cinnamon Tortie and White; Caramel Tortie and White; Si-Rex (Rex with the point pattern of the Siamese) and a range of colours following the Colourpoints (above: see Colourpoint Persians).

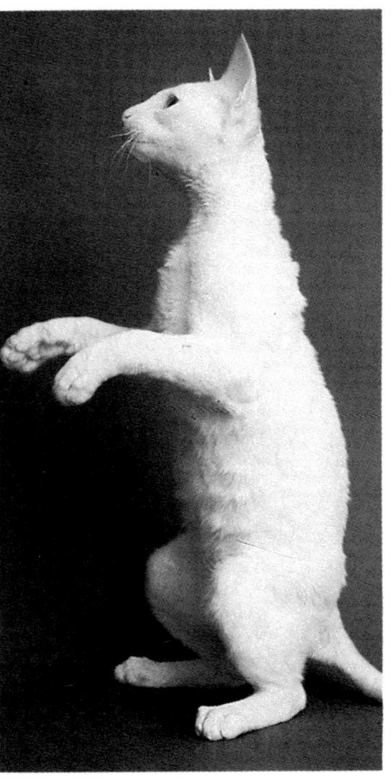

Patriaca Persil Ajax, a red-point Cornish Rex – the first ever of this breed appeared in a litter in Cornwall in 1950.

FOREIGN AND ORIENTAL SHORT-HAIRS SIAMESE TYPES

Varieties Havana, Foreign Lilac, Foreign White, Foreign Black, Foreign Blue, Foreign Red, Oriental Tortie (Black), Foreign Cream, Oriental Blue Tortie, Oriental Chocolate Tortie, Oriental Lilac Tortie, Foreign Cinnamon, Oriental Cinnamon Tortie, Foreign Caramel, Oriental Caramel Tortie.

Other Varieties

Oriental Spotted Tabby OST Brown (Black), OST Blue, OST Chocolate, OST Lilac, OST Red, OST Cream, OST Cinnamon, OST Black Silver, OST Blue Silver, OST

Chocolate Silver, OST Lilac Silver, OST Red Silver, OST Cream Silver, OST Cinnamon Silver.

Oriental Classic Tabby OCT Brown (Black) and a range of colours following the Oriental Spotted Tabby list (*above*).

Oriental Smoke Oriental Black Smoke, and Oriental Smoke range of colours covering Blue, Chocolate, Lilac, Red, Cream and Cinnamon.

Oriental Shaded Oriental Black Shaded and a range of colours following the Oriental Smoke (above).

Oriental Mackerel Tabby Oriental Mackerel Tabby Brown (Black) and a range of colours following the Oriental Spotted Tabby (*above*).

Oriental Ticked Tabby Oriental Ticked Tabby Brown (Black) and a range of colours following the Oriental Spotted Tabby (above).

Oriental Tipped Oriental Black Tipped and a range of colours following the Oriental Spotted Tabby (above) from Blue – Cinnamon.

Angora

The beautiful silky-coated cat which first came to Europe from

The Oriental Spotted Tabby is a result of a breeding programme in the early 70s to create a cat resembling the Ancient Egyptian breed.

Originally from Angora (Ankara) in Turkey, at the end of the 19th century a special breeding programme at Ankara Zoo saved the Angora from extinction.

Turkey two or three centuries ago took its name from Turkey's capital, Angora (now Ankara). But the breed almost disappeared, even in Turkey, in favour of the heavier Persian cat, and it was not until the early 1960s that the breed was re-established in the west in the United States from four cats taken there, with permission, from Turkey.

The Angora has only recently been recognized as a breed in Britain, its recognized colour range following that of the Manx. Other varieties of Angora recognized are: Cinnamon, Caramel, Cinnamon Torties, Caramel Tortie, Colourpointed (and a range of colours), Brown Shaded (and a range of Shaded Angora), Brown (Black) Mackerel Tabby (and a range of Mackerel Tabby Angora), Brown (Black) Ticked Tabby (and a range of Ticked Tabby Angora), and an Angora variant – the short-haired progeny of a mating with at least one Angora parent.

Burmese

The Burmese, though clearly a cat of foreign-style elegance, must never be thought of as a Siamese-type cat, even though it is believed to have originated as a hybrid between a Siamese and a dark-coated cat. Today's Burmese is distinctly individual, being a medium length cat, neither extremely Oriental nor cobbily short-hair in appearance. Its short, fine hair should have a glossy texture with the smoothness of satin.

Burmese varieties recognized in Britain are: Brown, Blue, Chocolate, Lilac, Red, Brown Tortie, Cream, Blue Tortie, Chocolate Tortie and Lilac Tortie.

In the United States, where the Burmese breed was first developed, a much smaller colour range is recognized. The Cat Fanciers Association recognizes only the original Brown, called Sable. Other associations recognize the blue, chocolate and lilac varieties, calling them Blue, Champagne and Platinum.

Siamese

Siamese cats came to the West as

Pangur Ban, Siamese kitten. At the turn of the century a writer predicted that the Siamese 'is never likely to be common, as the cats are delicate in this country'. Today it is perhaps the most popular pedigree breed.

gifts to British and American consuls in Bangkok from the Siamese royal household in the 1880s, though they had been seen in Britain in the 1870s, having perhaps been smuggled out of Siam, for the Siamese regarded the cat as near sacred. The short-haired cat with the distinctive colour points on its creamy coat was a temple cat, kept to guard Buddhist temples and royal palaces. It is thought that the breed may have originated, possibly as a mutation of a more traditionally patterned cat, even further east than Siam.

The first Siamese cats in Britain had a more rounded head and rather less slim and elegant body than the present ideal. They also tended to have kinked tails and sometimes a squint, both of which 'defects' have now been eliminated by careful breeding.

Siamese colour points recognized by the GCCF in the UK are:
Seal Point, Blue Point, Chocolate Point, Lilac Point, Seal Tabby Point, Blue Tabby Point, Chocolate Tabby Point, Lilac Tabby Point, Red Tabby Point, Cream Tabby Point, Red Point, Seal Blue Tortie Point, Chocolate Tortie Point, Lilac Tortie Point, Tortie Point, Cream Point, Seal Tortie Tabby Point, Blue Tortie Tabby Point, Chocolate Tortie Tabby Point, Lilac Tortie Tabby Point.

In North America the Red, Cream, Tabby and Tortie Points are not recognized as varieties of Siamese by all associations, some of which call these cats Colorpoint Shorthairs (not to be confused with the British Colourpoints, which the Americans call Himalayans).

Cats derived from the Siamese, but not recognized as Siamese

Balinese cats, although only recently recognized by the GCCF, are among the most striking and affectionate of breeds.

varieties, are: the Foreign White, a cat with the looks of a Siamese but with a completely white coat; the Foreign Black (Ebony Oriental Short-hair in America), a variety developed from the Seal Point Siamese; the Foreign Lilac (Lavender Oriental Short-hair or, sometimes, Foreign Lavender in America), a Siamese type with a solid lilac coat, that is, a frost grey with a pinkish tone, and green eyes rather than the Siamese blue; and the Havana (Havana Brown in America), which is a Chocolate Brown Siamese type, with a solid rich brown and glossy coat. Except for the Havana, all these cats are grouped under the general title of Oriental Short-hairs in North America.

Balinese
This is a long-haired foreign type derived from the Siamese, though as the result of a natural mutation rather than from controlled breeding. The Balinese has the general body shape of a Siamese, the same vivid blue eyes with an oriental slant, and colour pointing on its soft, silky coat. The Balinese was first taken up in North America, and is now also accepted in the UK, where the GCCF's recognized varieties, which have had championship status since June 1986, are:
Seal Point, Blue Point, Chocolate Point, Lilac Point, Red Point, Seal Tortie Point, Cream Point, Blue Tortie Point, Chocolate Tortie Point, Lilac Tortie Point, Blue Tabby Point, Chocolate Tabby Point, Lilac Tabby Point, Red Tabby Point, Seal Tortie Tabby Point, Cream Tabby Point, Blue Tortie Tabby Point, Chocolate Tortie Tabby Point, Lilac Tortie Tabby Point, short-haired progeny of a

mating with at least one Balinese parent (Balinese variant).

Cats from North America

Cat breeding in North America has taken many different paths from the business in Britain, developing new varieties and colours as well as quite different breeds. Even breeds, such as the Exotic Short-hair, at first glance much the same on both sides of the Atlantic, turn out to have differences in conformation and style. Other breeds which began the same have diverged over several generations of separate breeding. The American Havana Brown, for instance, stems from Havanas imported from Britain but has developed into a different, more rounded cat.

Some American cats, although not officially recognized in Britain, are still well-known and even sought after by fanciers:

American Wire-Hair
This is a short-haired cat with a coarse, wiry coat, like that of a Wire-Hair Terrier. On its head and ears the hair is tightly curled. The variety appeared as a mutant among an otherwise ordinary short-hair litter on a farm in New York State in the mid-1960s. Not long before this two cats with wiry coats had appeared on a building site in Britain and were exhibited at the National Cat Club Show.

Bombay
Another cat recently accepted for showing in the US but not recognized in the UK. This handsome cat is a cross between an American Short-hair and a Burmese. Its coat is black and shiny like patent leather.

Calico
Generally, this is the equivalent of the British Tortoiseshell, though some American associations recognize a coat pattern that is basically white with tri-colour patches and one that has black and red, but no cream, on a white ground.

Cymric
Meaning 'Welsh', this is the Canadian name of a tailless cat known in the United States as a

Bombay – so called because they look like miniature versions of the black leopard of India.

Cats are, by nature, very good mothers. **Below:** *A mother tabby cuddles her two-week old kitten while* **right** *a seven-week old kitten discovers the joys of playing with mum's whiskers.*

Whether jumping down or up, cats move with balletic grace and ease.

Above: *Marchaze Aztec Warrier, a very handsome Oriental Spotted Tabby, is the Supreme Cat Champion for 1988 (Marc Henrie).*
Left: *This new, stained-glass window for Salisbury Cathedral is the first ever to depict a moggie. Ginge, the Cathedral's beloved tom cat, is seen looking over the shoulder of Salisbury's first bishop, Richard Poore, as he lay the Cathedral's foundation stone in 1220. (© Dean and Chapter of Salisbury.)*
Right: *The British Blue or Chartreux was supposedly bred by Carthusian monks and was originally a native of France.*

Right: *The classic rolling on the back is a form of greeting which shows complete trust and is guaranteed to melt the heart of any cat lover.*

With their inherent curiosity cats are natural explorers. **Above:** *Two Abyssinian kittens show a keen interest in the garden while,* **below**, *this little tabby probably wishes he had stayed at home.*

Above: *Kittens love to play together, however when it comes to food sibling affection is forgotten!*

Below left: *The average cat can, and frequently does, sleep for 18 hours a day.*
Below right: *Cats come in all shapes and sizes as this sleek Havanna and fluffy Colourpoint illustrate.*

The colour of cats' eyes varies greatly, from soft green to piercing blue and vibrant orange and even a combination, as seen in the odd-eyed white. **Below:** *The familiar eerie glow of cats' eyes in the dark is created by a special layer of iridescent cells called the tapetum.*

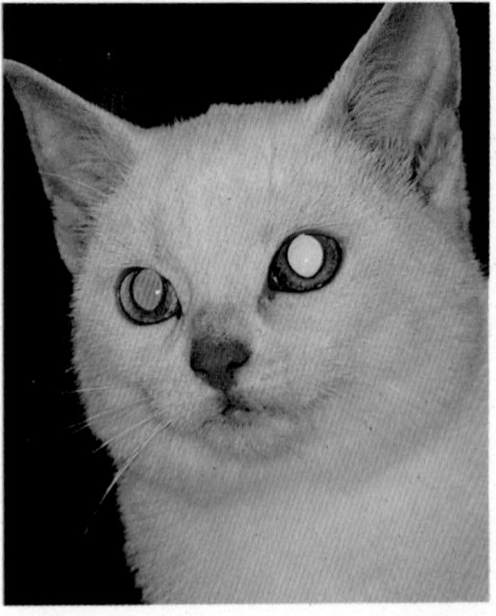

Manx Long-hair. As the name implies, the cat's hair is markedly longer and softer than that of the normal Manx. It was developed in North America in the late 1960s from long-haired kittens which appeared in the litters of normal Manx cats with pedigrees traceable back for several generations. The Cymric is missing its final spine/tail vertebrae and has the longer back legs and the same general body style as its short-hair relation.

Maine Coon

This popular and handsome long-hair is thought to have resulted from interbreeding at least a hundred years ago between an imported Angora and local New England cats, themselves brought to America by early settlers. The 'Maine' part of its name is obvious – the eastern seaboard state where it originated – but the 'Coon' comes from folklore, from the misguided belief that the cat was the result of a

Maine Coon – strong, attractive, adaptable and amiable.

The Tonkinese is a handsome and affectionate cat, the result of crossing American Burmese and Siamese cats.

cross between a raccoon and a domestic cat. The cat's coat is rugged, rather than very long, and comes in a wide range of colours and patterns.

Ragdoll
Another long-haired cat, the Ragdoll is a large, unusually placid individual rather like the Birman in looks. The first Ragdolls were kittens in a litter born to a cat who had recently been injured, and were all very limp and relaxed – hence the name Ragdoll. As adults, Ragdolls tend to show little reaction to things, even to illness, and must be watched carefully, since they may not tell people if anything is wrong.

Tonkinese
This elegant though fairly sturdy cat is the result of crossing American Burmese and Siamese cats, the differences between which are more marked than they are between the British or European breeds. A fairly recent breed, the Tonkinese is already available in the US in several colour varieties.

Quirky cats

Genetic mutation, coupled with careful breeding, has produced a medley of distinctive features among cats. Here are some of the extremes.

The lost tail The Manx cat has no tail at all; the vertebrae which in other cats start to form the tail at the end of the spine are completely missing from the Manx. Among the many legends accounting for this lack of tail which is, of course, genetic, perhaps the most picturesque is the one which has the Manx arriving so late to board the Ark that Noah accidentally shut the door on its tail. Apart from the completely tailless Manx, other varieties are recognized. In Britain,

these are the Stumpy, or Short-tailed Manx and the Tailed Manx. In the United States some cat fancy organisations recognise the Rumpy (tailless), Riser (in which a small number of tail vertebrae can be felt), Stubby (with a distinct, moveable short tail), Longy (the tail is longer but not full length) and the Tailed Manx.

The cat with the pom-pom tail
This is the Japanese Bobtail, an

From the series One Hundred Views of Ido *by Andō Hirōshige (1797–1858), featuring the Japanese Bobtail, ubiquitous in Japanese art and sculpture.*

ancient breed known in Japan – where it occurs naturally – for centuries. It is the cat seen over and over again in Japanese art and sculpture, often with a paw raised in a gesture of welcome. The cat gets its English name from its very short, 2–5 in (6–13 cm) long, fluffy tail, which looks even shorter than it is because it is carried crookedly and because it ends in a long-haired 'pom-pom'.

The Devon Rex has little or no whiskers and some are bald.

The curliest hair and the crinkliest whiskers These belong to the Cornish and Devon Rex cats, two genetically quite separate breeds of cat which appeared within ten years of each other in England's West Country in 1959 and 1969. Both cats have hair which seems permed, or crimped, and there is a complete absence of the long guard hairs found in other cats. The Cornish Rex's coat is curly, whereas the Devon Rex's is wavy. Even the Rex's whiskers and eyebrows are curly, an effect not seen in America's curliest-coated cat, the American Wire-Hair. This cat has very coarse, medium-length hair on its head, back, sides and the top edge of its tail.

The case of the disappearing hair In Ontario, Canada in 1966 a cat gave birth, among a normal litter, to a hairless cat. Now the hairless cat is an established variety in North America, called the Sphynx or Canadian Hairless. The Sphynx, which has a covering of almost imperceptible down, but no eyebrows or whiskers, is not recognized by the British cat fancy nor by several of the American cat fancy organisations.

A hairless cat known at the beginning of the century, but now completely disappeared, was the Mexican Hairless. In 1902, one of these cats was owned by a man in New Mexico, who said it was the last of the Aztec's breed of cat. He was not able to breed from it, and the type died out.

The cat with bent-over ears This is the Scottish Fold, its name derived from the fact that the forward-curving, or dropped ears appeared as a genetic mutation in a cat born in Perthshire, Scotland, in

Completely hairless, including eyebrows and whiskers, the coat of the Sphynx cat is said to feel like suede.

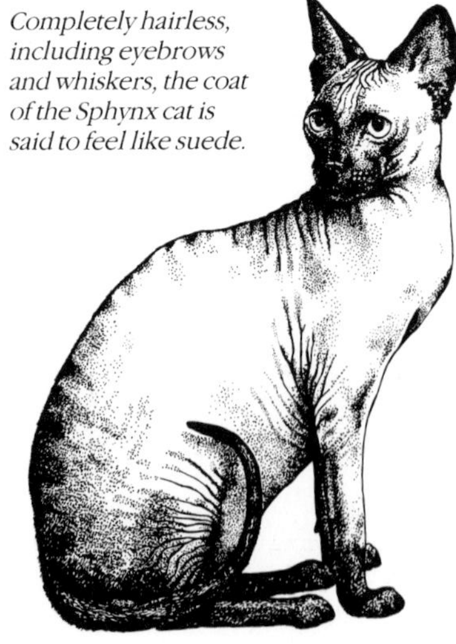

The first Scottish Fold kitten was discovered in Perthshire, Scotland, in 1961 by a shepherd.

1961. The cat was bred from and the breed established, which did not happen to the only other drop-ear cat known in Britain this century. (Drop-ear cats were known in China at least as early as the 18th century.) The Scottish Fold is not yet accepted as a breed in Britain, partly because there has not been sufficient time to assess how susceptible the drop-ears may be to infection or how they will affect the cat's hearing.

The dog-faced cat There is a well-established variety of long-hair cat in the United States with a face like a Pekinese. This is the Peke-Faced Persian, so-called because its face has the distinctive features of the popular dog: the pushed-in front-face look, with retroussé nose and heavy wrinkles on the muzzle and from the corners of the eyes. The cat's big, round eyes are also slightly protruding, though this is not so marked as in the Pekinese. The Peke-Face is not approved by the British cat fancy; the extreme shortness of the nose may cause breathing difficulties, there is a danger of jaw deformity, and the tear ducts may become blocked, though careful breeding should guard against all of these.

The Peke-Faced Persian has been bred to resemble the dog, and care must be taken not to over-develop characteristics which could be harmful to the cat.

The spottiest cat This is the Spotted Short-Hair, its name deriving from its handsome spotted coat. Although cats with spotted coats were known to the Ancients – in the Egyptian *Book of the Dead* Ra is shown as a spotted cat slaying the serpent of the dark world – today's Spotted Short-Hair is a very recent variety which has been seriously developed only since the mid-1960s. The spots in the coat must be well balanced and rounded; broken stripes or narrow markings like the tabby will not do.

Also spotted, but tending slightly more towards the tabby, is the coat of the Egyptian Mau, or Oriental Spotted Tabby, a breed created in a conscious attempt to revive the cat type known to the Ancient Egyptians.

A cat from the Ancient world? Some people claim that today's Abyssinian cat, brought to Britain from Ethiopia in the 1860s, is descended directly from the cats of the Pharoahs. Others say that it is the handsome result of a carefully selective breeding programme. Either way, the Abyssinian's 'agouti' coat, in which each hair is 'ticked' or marked with two or three bands of colour, is similar to that of the African Wild Cat, and its general form is very like that of cats in Ancient Egyptian sculptures and paintings.

Cat shows

A HISTORY

Cat writer and show judge Angela Sayer identifies the very first cat show ever recorded as an event which took place at St Giles Fair, Winchester, England in 1598, towards the end of Elizabeth I's reign.

The first modern, 'benched' cat show took place at the Crystal Palace in London in July 1871. The show was the brainchild of Mr Harrison Weir, a Fellow of the Horticultural Society, an artist and a cat lover. He conceived the idea of the show as a way of focusing interest on the different cat breeds and promoting sound breeding practices. About 160 cats were entered. Two years later a second cat show was held in London, this time at Alexandra Palace, and another in Birmingham.

The first cat show in Scotland was held in Edinburgh in 1875 and attracted 560 cats. A special attraction at this show was a cat which had been rescued from the ninth floor of a building after a fire.

The first properly organised cat show in the United States, complete with show benches, was held in Madison Square Garden, New York, in 1895. These days, over 400 cat shows a year are held across the USA.

The world's largest annual cat show is held by the National Cat Club. The Club, originally a registering body for pedigree cats, was formed in England in 1887. The Club's 90th Championship Show was held at Olympia in London in 1985 and attracted over 2,000 entries. There were also 26 vets and 120 judges on duty.

SHOW TITLES

The titles or awards presented at cat shows are called **Champion** and **Grand Champion**. In the *United Kingdom* a Champion is a cat winning three gold challenge certificates at three different shows under three separate judges; a Grand Champion is a cat winning three Grand Challenge certificates at three shows under three judges. In the *United States* a Champion is a cat that has won six winners'

ribbons under at least four different judges; a Grand Champion is a Champion cat that has been awarded the equivalent of seven Grand Ribbons by accumulating points in Best Champion competitions. In both the UK and US cats may not bear the name Champion until the relevant registering body has approved the title and checked the cat's breeding.

Premier and **Grand Premier** are equivalent titles for neutered or spayed cats.

SHOW CATEGORIES
In the UK there are something like 90 cat shows held under GCCF rules every year. GCCF-sponsored shows fall into three categories: **Championship** shows, **Sanctions**, and **Exemptions**. *Exemptions* may be introductory shows run by clubs newly affiliated to the GCCF; cat show sections in larger shows, such as Agricultural Society shows; or shows by non-affiliated clubs. For these shows, the GCCF rules concerning such matters as the number of judges present are not necessarily strictly adhered to, and the general atmosphere is relaxed; GCCF certificates are not awarded. *Sanctions* are, in a way, dress rehearsals for full Championship shows, and the GCCF rules are strictly adhered to, though no certificates are awarded. For affiliated clubs, two Exemption shows successfully completed generally lead to a Sanctions show.

The 1986 Supreme Grand Champion. Pannaduloa Blazer at the National Cat Club Show at Olympia, a male Red Point Siamese owned and bred by Mr John Hansson.

The *Championship* shows are, as the name implies, the most important show for a pedigree cat to appear in; here the all-important GCCF Challenge and premier certificates are awarded. The Mecca for these certificate winners is the GCCF's annual Supreme Show, usually held in May towards the end of the cat show year, which runs from June to May. At this show are chosen the Supreme Grand Champions of the British cat world.

SHOW CLASSES

Prizes may be awarded in a great variety of classes at British cat shows. The major classes are, of course, the Open Classes for adult cats and kittens (that is, cats up to nine months old) of the recognized breeds. At shows governed by GCCF rules, other classes may be:

Senior cats two years old and over.
Junior cats under two years old.
Breeders kittens bred by the exhibitor.
Notice cats and kittens which have not won a First Prize under GCCF rules.
Limit for cats that have won not more than four first prizes.
Special limit for cats that have won not more than two first prizes.
Debutante for cats and kittens that have not been exhibited before under GCCF rules.
Maiden for cats that have not won a First, Second or Third prize under GCCF rules.
Novice exhibitor for cats whose owners have never won a money prize under GCCF rules (the cat itself may have been a prize winner).
Radius for exhibitors living within a specified distance of the exhibition hall.
Champion of Champions a class for full Champions only.
Premier of Premiers a class for full Premiers only.
Household pets classes for domestic pets and non-pedigree cats, which could include such classes as 'Owned by a child under 16 years', or 'glossiest coat', or even 'with most appealing expression'.

The National Cat Club emblem designed by Louis Wain.

Top cat clubs

The first cat club, the **National Cat Club** was founded in England in 1887 by Harrison Weir, the man who had organised the world's first cat show in 1871. The National Cat Club was the cat fancy's first registering body, keeping a register of pedigree cats, granting championships, and issuing the first stud book (in 1893). The club's annual show at Olympia in London is still the biggest of its kind in the world.
Address The Secretary, The Laurels, Rocky Lane, Wendover, Bucks.

Among the various cat clubs and fanciers' associations formed in the UK round the turn of the century, one of the earliest breed clubs was the **Siamese Cat Club**, founded in 1901. Today in the UK, among the 94 clubs affiliated to the country's main cat fancy association, the GCCF, 49 are breed clubs; if your cat is an Abyssinian or a White Persian, a Balinese or a Burmese, a Cameo or a Korat, a Havana or a Rex, then there is a cat club specifically for you.
Addresses Available from the GCCF (see below).

The **Governing Council of the Cat Fancy** (GCCF) is the UK's oldest existing registering body, and the largest. It was formed in 1910 to provide an 'umbrella' organisation under which the various cat clubs could come together to agree matters of interest to the cat fancy in general. The GCCF took over the registering and other functions of the National Cat Club.
Address 4–6 Penel Orlieu, Bridgwater, Somerset TA6 3PG.

Much more recent is the **Cat Association of Great Britain** (CA), founded in 1983 as an alternative to the GCCF. The CA is run entirely by its members and its register of cats includes pedigree, half pedigree and non-pedigree animals.
Address CA National Information Office, Hunting Grove, Lowfield Heath, Crawley, West Sussex RH11 0PY.

The largest cat fancy organisation in the world is the **Federation Internationale Feline** (FIFe). Registering bodies from most of the countries of Western Europe are affiliated to FIFe, which also has affiliates in many other countries round the world. FIFe has a judges' commission responsible for studying new breeds and standards, modifying them where necessary, and for regulating the stud book; a show commission responsible for seeing that shows are managed efficiently and show rules correctly applied, and a disciplinary commission which hears complaints and problems from its member organisations and arbitrates in disputes.
Address General Secretary, 33 Rue Duquesnoy, B1000, Brussels, Belgium.

The most fragmented cat organisation in the world is probably that of the United States where there are no fewer than nine registering bodies.

The oldest cat registry in America is the **American Cat Association** (ACA), active since at least 1899, and operating in the south-east and south-west of the United States. Address: The Secretary, ACA, 10065 Foothill Boulevard, Lake View Terrace, California 91342, USA. The country's largest registry is the **Cat Fanciers' Association** (CFA), with affiliates in Canada and Japan. The CFA's annual yearbook is a major cat fancy publication. Address: Executive Manager, CFA, 1309 Allaire Avenue, Ocean, New Jersey 07712, USA.

The USA's youngest cat association, **The International Cat Association** (TICA) also has affiliates in Canada and Japan and is growing fast. Address: TICA, 211 East Oliver, Suite 208, Burbank, California 91502, USA.

The Cat in the Language

From our earliest childhood and nursery days we encounter the cat in nursery rhymes, in countless stories and poems and in everyday expressions and phrases.

Cat dictionary

Agouti – a particular coat pattern in cats, in which individual hairs are colour banded, giving a ticked effect in the coat. It is a wild-cat type of coat pattern.

Ailurophilia – the love of cats.

Ailurophobia – extreme dislike of cats. When the feeling is really acute, people may sweat, turn pale, and experience nausea and hysteria. Both this word and 'ailurophilia' come from the Greek word for a ferret, *ailauros*, the connection lying in the fact that the Greeks kept ferrets as rat-catchers.

Angora – originally the name given in Europe to the first cats with long hair, which were thought to have come from Turkey, whose capital was Angora (Ankara).

Cat – this common European word, found in similar form in almost all European languages seems to have been around since at least the 4th century AD, and may have derived originally from the Nubian word *kadis*, being carried along the great Mediterranean and European trade routes with the cat itself.

Catmatic – a word to watch out for, since it has just been invented by a man from Seattle, USA. He coined it as an opposite to 'dogmatic' and it means 'to pussyfoot around'.

Cyprus – a word once used in parts of Britain to mean a 'tabby' cat. It derived from the name for a type of fabric, known in the 17th and 18th centuries, which was a cloth made of silk and hair, with wavy lines in it, imported from Cyprus.

Felinophile – a cat lover, from the Latin word for a cat, (all kinds, not just domestic), *Felis*.

Grimalkin – a word often applied to cats, sometimes as another word for 'cat', sometimes as the name of a particular cat. It is said to derive from the name of a foul fiend, Malkin (this name itself being a diminutive of Maud or Matilda), superstitiously associated with witches. The cat's perceived role in medieval times as a witches' familiar or even a witch transformed into a cat shape led to its being called Grimalkin (from the French word 'gris') or Graymalkin.

Kindle – a litter of kittens.

Kitten – a young cat, aged up to 9 months in Britain, 8 months in the USA.

Mau – the delightfully onomatopoeic Egyptian word for a cat; means 'to see' in English. The name is now given to a variety of cat (the Egyptian Mau or Oriental Spotted Tabby), specifically bred to look like the cats of Ancient Egypt.

Puss – a call word for cats, thought to be derived from the name of Egyptian cat goddess Pasht, or Bastet.

Queen – a mother cat; a female cat used for breeding.

Tabby – another descriptive word derived from a fabric, this word describing a particular coat pattern in cats, comes from 'tabbi' or 'atabi' silk, which was imported from Attabiya, part of old Baghdad, where it was made, around the 17th and 18th centuries. The silk was a black and white fabric with a watered effect.

CAT COLLOQUIALISMS

Most phrases involving cats have been around for centuries, so it is not always easy to pinpoint their origins.

Alley cat – a person without proper antecedents.

Another breed of cat – something else again.

Bear cat – a person who is hard to reason with,.

Cat – several meanings, depending on context. The word can mean a spiteful woman, a jazz fan or musician, or be 'Black' slang for 'man'.

A cat and dog life – a life of constant bickering and ill-tempered discord.

Cat and mouse – toying with someone, usually for unkind or even cruel reasons.

To cat around – to live an aimless, unco-ordinated life.

Catbird – common name of several birds with cat-like cries, especially *Dumetella carolincasis*, a North American songbird whose call sounds like a cat mewing, and several common birds of Australia.

Cat burglar – a nimble thief, good at scaling walls and roofs.

Catcall – a raucous, disapproving whistle or cry.

Cat's cradle – a string game for agile fingers.

Cat-eyes – able to see well in the dark.

Cat's eyes – precious or semi-precious gems, forms of chrysoberyl or quartz, which have a changing lustre. Also road markers which reflect car lights, invented by an Englishman, Percy Shaw.

Cat's foot – to live under the cat's foot is to submit to petticoat government, to be hen-pecked.

Cat house – in our time, a brothel; in earlier centuries a moveable penthouse used in sieges.

Catkins – deciduous fluffy-looking flower bracts of trees such as the willow or birch, and looking like small cats' tails.

Alice meets the grinning Cheshire Cat.

Catlap – usually milk or weak tea; something fit only for cats to drink.

Catnap – a short, light doze.

Cat's melody – squalling.

The cat's meow – was coined by the American cartoonist and prolific dreamer-up of catchphrases, Thomas A. Dorgan (1877–1929), whose work, signed TAD, appeared in many American newspapers. Dating from about the same time in America and with much the same meaning are *the cat's whiskers* and *the cat's pyjamas* – something special or first rate.

Cat's paw – a dupe or tool.

Cat's sleep – a sham sleep; sleeping with one eye open.

Catty – spiteful.

Catwalk – a narrow walkway between the fly doors above a stage; any narrow walkway, as on the bridge of a ship; the raised platform along which models walk to show off the clothes at a fashion show.

Cat wash – a lick and a promise.

The cat's got his tongue – he's speechless, though probably not for long.

Cool cat – laid back, refusing to become excited.

Copy cat – one who, lacking originality, copies others.

Enough to make a cat laugh – ridiculously silly.

Enough to make a cat speak – tongue-loosening, as in alcohol.

Fat cat – person richly endowed with money and goods.

Fight like Kilkenny cats – to fight until both sides have lost everything. The phrase arises out of the activities of a garrison of Hessean troops at Kilkenny, Ireland, during the Irish rebellion of 1798 and the sport of a group of soldiers with a couple of cats.

Fight like cat and dog – no mere squabbling, this is serious physical fighting.

Fraidy cat – one who is frightened before he has any need to be.

Glamour puss – a glamorous lady.

Grin like a Cheshire Cat – a very wide grin, like that on the Cheshire cat in *Alice's Adventures in Wonderland.*

Hellcat – a bad-tempered, unmanageable woman.

Hep cat – a with-it, sharp-minded person.

Kitty-corner – to set something at an angle, across a corner.

Like a cat on hot bricks – jumpy, uneasy.

Looking like something the cat dragged in – unkempt, rough and unwashed.

Make the fur fly – start a fight.

Pickle-puss – a sour face.

Pussy foot – to approach a problem indecisively.

Put the cat among the pigeons – stir up trouble.

Raining cats and dogs – raining heavily.

Rub someone's fur the wrong way – to upset, irritate them.

Scaredy cat – a coward.

See which way the cat jumps – appraise a situation from all angles before acting.

The cat did it – to shift the blame elsewhere.

Tom cat – a man who chases women.

CAT ADAGE

The cat has been the subject of many common English-language proverbs. Here are a few, most of them with obvious meanings.

All cats have claws.

All cats love fish but fear to wet their paws. Used of people not caring to risk trouble to achieve desired ends.

At night/In the dark all cats are grey. This proverb, meaning that all men are undistinguished until they have made their mark, is found in several European languages.

Before the cat can lick his ear. Means 'never', since a cat can't lick his ear.

The best cats can lose a mouse.

A cat has nine lives. There are numerous variations on this universal saying: 'More lives than a cat', 'He's using up his nine lives', etc. The saying arises out of the cat's extraordinary ability to land on its feet – another useful cat-derived phrase.

A cat may look at a king.

Care killed the cat.

Curiosity killed the cat.

To let the cat out of the bag. Meaning to disclose a secret, this proverb derives from the old country trick of 'selling a pig in a poke' – the wise buyer would check if there was really a sucking pig in the bag; if it turned out not to be, he was letting the cat out of the bag.

Looks like a cat that has swallowed a canary.

Muffled cats catch no mice. Said of those who try to work in gloves to avoid getting dirty hands.

Not room to swing a cat. This saying probably derives from an 'amusement' of earlier centuries – to swing a cat, sometimes in a bag or sack, or even a leather bottle, as a mark for sportsmen to aim at – though it may also refer to the room needed to swing a cat o'nine tails.

As sick as a cat. Deriving from the cat's propensity to vomit, often in an effort to bring up fur balls, this saying refers specifically to a drunken man; the actual act of vomiting drunkenly was called 'shooting the cat'.

A singed cat avoids the fire.

Too old a cat to be fooled by a kitten.

To turn cat-in-pan. Meaning to turn traitor, or to be a turncoat, this phrase is thought to have derived from, not cats, but a French phrase, *tourner cote en pein*, meaning to change sides when in trouble.

What can you have of a cat but its skin? Derived from the fact that although the cat's fur might be of use to trim cloaks, no other part of the animal was of use.

When the cat's away the mice will play. Another saying common throughout Europe.

Who is 'she'? The cat's mother?

Who is to bell the cat? Or, who will risk his life for his neighbours? The saying refers to the fable of the mice seeking a way to warn themselves of the cat's approach. One mouse suggests hanging a bell round its neck. A wise mouse asks 'Who will undertake the task?'

Cats at sea

'Cat' has found its way into many nautical and shipboard names and phrases.

Many cat terms refer to ropes and tackle: *cat-block, cat falls, cat-harping, cat-head, cat-rigged, cat-roller, cat-stopper* and *cat-tail.*

Cat's paw is the sailors' term for the breeze that ripples the water during a calm and which is the first hint of a coming squall.

Cat o' nine tails was the nine-lashed whip used for floggings in the British navy and, later, the army.

To cat the anchor is the action of hanging the anchor on the cathead, a fitting on the ship's side from which the anchor hung clear of the ship's side.

A catboat is a small boat with one mast, set well forward, and with one sail extended by a gaff and boom (i.e. cat-rigged).

Cats in pub names

The Cat and Fiddle. Nothing at all to do with a musical cat, this pub name may have several derivations. Two are corruptions of French: 'Le Chat Infidéle' or 'The Unfaithful

Cat', 'Caton le fidéle' or 'Faithful Caton', a Governor of Calais. The most likely origin of the name is the nursery rhyme 'Hey Diddle Diddle'. The 'Cat and Fiddle' near Macclesfield in Cheshire is, says the *Good Pub Guide*, the highest English pub to stay open all year.

The Cat and Kittens refers to the different-sized pewter pots used for serving beer in pubs and alehouses. Stealing the pots was called 'cat and kitten sneaking'.

Other 'catty' pub names to be found in England include:

Black Cat
Cat (and Cats)
Cat Head (or Cat's Head)
Cat and Bagpipes
Cat and Cracker
Cat and Custard Pot
(also Cat and Mustard Pot)
Cat and Lion
Cat and Mutton
Cat and Tiger
Cat's Whisker
Cat in the Basket
Cat in the Cage
Cat in the Wall
Cat in the Well
Cat in the Window
Civet Cat
Ginger Tom
Laughing Cat
Mad Cat
Old Cat
Poplar Kitten
Puss in Boots
Rampant Cat
Red Cat
Romping Cat
Salutation and Cat
Squinting Cat
Tabby Cat
Whittington and His Cat
Whittington Cat

Cats in literature

Animal stories have been written from the earliest days of literature. Here are some of the cats whose stories have delighted readers over the years.

Aesop
Aesop, a Greek who seems to have lived in the mid 6th century BC, has had his fables rewritten many times since Caxton printed the first English edition in 1484. They include numerous cats, most of them seen as the villain of the piece. Cat fables by Aesop include: *The Cat and the Bat, The Cat and the Birds, The Cat and the Cock, The Cat and the Mice, The Cat and the Sparrows,* and *The Cat, The Monkey and the Chestnuts*

La Fontaine
Raminagrobis was a cat which featured in several of the *Fables* of Jean de la Fontaine (1621–95). In *The Cat, the Weasel and the Rabbit* Raminagrobis was asked to settle a dispute between the weasel and the rabbit. Feigning the deafness of old age, Raminagrobis asked the two animals to come closer; when they did, he grabbed them both and devoured them.

Raminagrobis the wily old cat from the Fables *of La Fontaine. Illustration by J.J. Grandville.*

Fairy Tales

Seventeenth-century French writer, Charles Perrault, was responsible for *Puss-in-Boots*, the wonderfully clever and sophisticated cat whose exploits in turning a low-born youth into the noble Marquis of Carabas and fit to marry a princess, proved so ideal for English pantomime as well as children's books. Perrault was perhaps inspired to write *Puss-in-Boots* by his knowledge of the magician cat, or *matagot*, in which the people of southern France firmly believed. These *matagots*, who were part of the folklore of other countries besides France, brought good luck to people who received them with kindness.

Dick Whittington, the most popular English cat fairy tale, is also a splendid subject for pantomime. Although Richard Whittington was a real person who became Lord Mayor of London three times around the turn of the 14th century, his cat was pure fairy tale and all sorts of origins have been suggested for him. Some say he was originally part of a story from 10th-century Persia, reaching England by way of Venice and medieval Europe, others suggested he was really the type of boat (a cat) which transported the Lord Mayor's trading ventures.

A cat fairy tale to reach English nurseries in the 19th century was *The Four Musicians of Bremen*, one of the stories of the German philologists and folklorists, Jacob and Wilhelm Grimm. The musicians were four animals, a donkey, a dog, a cat and a cock, too old to be of use to their owners, who found themselves a new life in Bremen by banding together to frighten a gang of robbers out of a house.

Puss-in-Boots, inspired by the magician cat of 17th-century southern France. Engraving by Gustave Doré (1832–83).

Alice's cats
Lewis Carroll gave Alice, heroine of his two most famous children's books, a cat of her own called Dinah, as well as putting the famous Cheshire Cat among the characters Alice met in Wonderland. By the time *Through the Looking Glass and What Alice Found There* was published in 1871 Dinah had acquired two kittens, Kitty and Snowdrop, who went through the Looking-glass world with Alice as the Red Queen and the White Queen.

The Cheshire Cat in *Alice's Adventures in Wonderland* could talk and he could vanish slowly, his wide grin disappearing last of all. Alice first encountered him in the Duchess's kitchen: 'Please would you tell me,' said Alice a little timidly . . . 'why your cat grins like that?' 'It's a Cheshire Cat,' said the Duchess, 'and that's why.' Not contented with this inadequate explanation, people have been trying ever since to discover the origins of Lewis Carroll's cat. A likely explanation for the name, accepted in early editions of *Brewer's Dictionary for Phrase and Fable*, is that Carroll had in mind a type of Cheshire cheese which was sold in a cat-shaped mould.

Although *Alice's Adventures in Wonderland* has been translated into many languages and has never been out of print since it was first published in 1865, it was not available for a time in China: the Chinese authorities censored the book in 1931 because they considered it wrong, even disastrous, that animals and human beings should be put on the same level and that animals should use human languages.

The world of Beatrix Potter

Beatrix Potter's cats are generally plump and fluffy pusses with large eyes and pretty faces, and must have been based on the real cats she knew in her home. The main 'cat' stories among Beatrix Potter's books are:

The Tale of Peter Rabbit (1900) was the first of her books to be published. It gave just a glimpse of Mr McGregor's elegant white cat – someone to be avoided, according to Peter's cousin, Benjamin.
The Tailor of Gloucester (1902) featured the lively cat Simpkin.
The Tale of Benjamin Bunny (1904) provided a different cat for Mr McGregor, a large and handsome animal who kept Peter and Benjamin trapped in a basket by lying on the lid.
Miss Moppet (1906) was a flighty little lady who spent most of the book teasing a mouse.
The Tale of Tom Kitten (1907) was about the three naughty kittens of Mrs Tabitha Twitchit – Moppet, Mittens and Tom Kitten.
The Tale of Samuel Whiskers (1908) had Tom Kitten in trouble again, this time with the rat Samuel Whiskers and his rather bad-tempered wife, who rolled Tom Kitten up in dough (hence the book's original title, *The Roly-Poly Pudding*.)
Ginger and Pickles (1909) in which Ginger was a marmalade farm cat and Pickles a terrier. They ran a village shop, giving too many of their customers unlimited credit to compete with Mrs Tabitha Twitchit's shop.
The Tale of Johnny Town-Mouse (1918) provided the cook's kitchen with three kittens and a large cat, who had killed the canary, a crime for which Johnny Town-Mouse was blamed.

Kipling's Cat

Rudyard Kipling's story *The Cat that Walked by Himself*, was one of a dozen which he told first to his children and then published in book form, called *Just So Stories for Little Children*, in 1902. Kipling's story told how the woman tamed the dog, the horse and the cow to serve her and Man, and how she and the Man almost, but not quite, tamed the cat: 'He will kill mice, and he will be kind to Babies . . . But when he had done that, and between times, and when the moon gets up and the night comes, he is the Cat that walks by himself, and all places are alike to him.'

The Marmalade Cat
Kathleen Hale based her drawings of Orlando, his wife, Grace, and their kittens, Pansy, Blanche and Tinkle, on her own cats. The first Orlando book, *Orlando the Marmalade Cat: A Camping Holiday*, was published in 1938 and the last, *Orlando the Marmalade Cat, and the Water Cats*, in 1972. Between these two came:

Orlando the Marmalade Cat: A trip Abroad (1939);
Orlando's Evening Out (1941);
Orlando's Home Life (1942);
Orlando Buys a Farm (1942);
Orlando's Silver Wedding (1944);
Orlando Becomes a Doctor (1944);
Orlando's Invisible Pyjamas (1947);
Orlando Keeps a Dog (1949);
Orlando the Judge (1950);
Orlando's Seaside Holiday (1952);
Orlando's Zoo (1954);
Orlando's Magic Carpet (1958);
The Frisky Housewife (1959);
Orlando Buys a Cottage (1963);
Orlando and the Three Graces (1965);
Orlando the Marmalade Cat Goes to the Moon (1968).

A ballet about Orlando was written and performed during the Festival of Britain in 1951.

20TH-CENTURY CLASSICS
The American writer, Paul Gallico has written two fine cat books, which may be read with equal pleasure by children and adults alike. *Jennie* (1950) and *Thomasina* (1957) both featured cats who became unforgettably real and alive in Gallico's compassionate, loving writing.

Dr Seuss's *Cat in the Hat* (1957) was the first in a series of beginners' reading books by an American whose real name is Theodor Seuss Giesel. His books marked new ground in children's cat books, for his tone was that of a comic book and the humour was often violent.

In great contrast was Sheila Burnford's *The Incredible Journey* (1960), a moving, if rather sentimental tale based on the true story of two dogs and a cat who trekked over 300 miles of wild country in north-western Ontario to return to their owners' home. The cat involved was a Siamese called Tao. The story was filmed by Walt Disney in 1963.

A very jolly witch's cat to appear more recently in children's books has been Mog, a main character in Helen Nicoll's tales of Meg and her cat Mog, all illustrated with great vigour by Jan Pienkowski. The first book about these two was *Meg and Mog* (1972) followed by *Meg's Eggs* (1972), *Meg at Sea* (1973) and *Meg on the Moon* (1973).

The illustrations have been an essential part of many of the best children's cat books published in recent years. Some of the best-selling have been Richard Scarry's many books featuring the boy cat Huckle and his family, William Mayne's *Calico Cat,* illustrated by Nicola Bayley, Graham Oakley's *Church Cat*, and Shirley Hughes' *Chips and Jessie*, in which the cat was called Albert and the dog Barkis.

Nursery rhyme cats

Here, the origins of some of the most familiar cats of all are sought, with the help of the *Oxford Dictionary of Nursery Rhymes*, which discusses most of the rhymes quoted.

Hey diddle diddle, *the best-known of all nonsense poems.*

Great A, little a.
Bouncing B,
The cat's in the cupboard
And she can't see me.

There are several versions of this nursery rhyme, of which this one is believed to have originated in the 18th century as a poem to help teach children the alphabet.

A cat came fiddling out of a barn,
With a pair of bagpipes under her arm;
She could sing nothing but, Fiddle cum fee,
The mouse has married the bumble bee.
Pipe cat, dance mouse;
We'll have a wedding at our good house.

Various forms of this rhyme are known, the earliest dating back to about 1740; the theme of the cat fiddling, or playing some other musical instrument, is much older, stretching right back to the Ancient Egyptians and their mystical musical instrument, the Sistrum, the symbol of the world's harmony associated with the sacred cat gods of Egypt.

Ding, dong, bell
Pussy's in the well.
Who put her in?
Little Johnny Green.
Who pulled her out?
Little Tommy Stout.
What a naughty boy was that
To try to drown poor pussy cat,
Who never did him any harm
And killed the mice in his father's barn.

Well-known in the time of Shakespeare, who alluded to it in several of his plays, this rhyme has been known to children for more than four centuries.

Hey diddle diddle
The cat and the fiddle
The cow jumped over the moon;
The little dog laughed to see such fun
And the dish ran away with the spoon.

The best-known of all nonsense poems, this has also been part of

the language for at least four centuries. Its origins are unknown, though the *Oxford Dictionary of Nursery Rhymes* says that there are some grounds for believing that it may have grown out of the game of 'cat' (trap ball) played in inns, and the fiddle (or music in general), once provided in English inns.

This is the house that Jack built . . .
This is the cat
That killed the rat
That ate the malt
That lay in the house that Jack built.

The best-known accumulative rhyme in the language, the story of Jack and his house first appeared in print in 1755 in *Nurse Truelove's New Year's Gift*, published by Newbery.

Three little kittens they lost their mittens,
And they began to cry . . .

This rhyme first appeared in a collection called *New Nursery Rhymes for All Good Children*, collected by a New England children's writer, Eliza Foller. She is not thought to have written the rhyme, which she called 'traditional'.

The cattie sits in the kiln-rug.
Spinning, spinning;
Any by came a little wee mousie,
Rinning, rinning.

A genuine rhyme from the nursery, this is part of the oral tradition of Scotland and northern England, having been told by countless mothers and nurses to their 'bairns'. It was collected by the writer and publisher, Robert Chambers, in the first half of the 19th century.

Six little mice sat down to spin;
Pussy passed by and she peeped in.
Pussy passed by and she peeped in.
What are you doing my little men?
Weaving coats for gentlemen.

This rhyme, probably dating from the mid-19th century, was very much in Beatrix Potter's mind when she wrote *The Tailor of Gloucester.*

I love little pussy,
Her coat is so warm,
And if I don't hurt her
She'll do me no harm.

Often ascribed, wrongly, to Jane Taylor, author of *Twinkle Twinkle Little Star*, this poem first appeared in the United States, being published in *The Child's Song Book* in Boston in 1830.

Pussy cat, pussy cat, where have you been?
I've been to London to look at the queen.
Pussy cat, pussy cat, what did you there?
I frightened a little mouse under her chair.

Tradition has it that this rhyme was based on a real incident, and that the queen involved was Elizabeth I.

Poetic cats

'All your wondrous wealth of hair,
Dark and fair,
Silken-shaggy, soft and bright
As the clouds and beams of night,
Pays my reverent hand's caress
Back with friendlier gentleness.'

Algernon Swinburne, To a cat

There are many fine cat poems, of course, and it is interesting to note how many of them were inspired, not by the *idea* of the cat, but by a real animal, usually the companion of the poet, or at least known to them.

One of the earliest English poems about a cat is, in fact, a translation of a poem originally written in Irish in the 8th century AD. The author was a monk who was a student and copier of manuscripts, his main companion his cat.

'I and Pangur Ban, my cat
'Tis a like task we are at;
Hunting mice is his delight,
Hunting words I sit all night.

Oftentimes a mouse will stray
In the hero Pangur's way;
Oftentimes my keen thought set
Takes a meaning in its net . . .'

Chaucer included in his *Manciple's Tale* a cat who, despite plenty of milk, tender meat and a silken bed . . .

'Anon he weyveth milk and flesch
and al,
And every deyntee that is in that
hous,
Suich appetit he hath to ete a
mous.'

The cat's next starring roles in English poetry did not come until the 18th century. First, there was Jeoffry, companion of **Christopher Smart** during his confinement in the notorious Bethlehem lunatic asylum, better known as Bedlam, in London. A large section of his great poem, *Jubilate Agno*, or *Rejoice in the Lamb: a Song from Bedlam*, was a litany of the cat's many virtues:

'For I will consider my cat Jeoffry.
For he is the servant of the living
God,
duly and daily serving him . . .
For having done duty and received
blessing
he begins to consider himself.
For this he performs in ten
degrees.
For first he looks upon his fore-
paws to see if they are clean.
For secondly he kicks up behind to
clear away there.
For thirdly he works it upon stretch
with the fore-paws extended.
For fourthly he sharpens his paws
by wood . . .

Living in the same period, but in a much grander household, was Selima, pet cat of **Horace Walpole**. When Selima's famous accident befell her, Horace Walpole passed the news of it to his good friend, the poet **Thomas Gray**. Gray replied with the mock-heroic *Ode on the Death of a Favourite Cat, Drowned in a Tub of Gold Fishes:*

'Twas on a lofty vase's side
Where China's gayest art had
dyed
The azure flowers that blow;
Demurest of the tabby kind,
The pensive Selima, reclined,
Gazed on the lake below . . .

Eight times emerging from the
flood
She mew'd to ev'ry wat'ry God,
Some speedy aid to send.
No dolphin came, no Nereid
stirr'd;
Nor cruel Tom, nor Susan heard.
A fav'rite has no friend!

From hence, ye beauties,
undeceived,
Know, one false step is ne'er
retrieved,
And be with caution bold.
Not all that tempts your wand'ring
eyes
And heedless hearts is lawful prize;
Nor all that glisters, gold.

Shelley indulged in a rather inflated style, though he was describing his own cat:

'O bard-like spirit! beautiful and swift!
Sweet lover of pale night;
The dazzling glory of thy gold-tinged tail,
Thy whisker-wavering lips!

Keats' cat sonnet was also addressed to a real cat – *Mrs Reynolds' Cat:*

'Cat! who pass'd thy grand climacteric,
How many mice and rats hast in thy days
Destroy'd? How many tit-bits stolen?
Gaze
With those bright languid segments green,
and prick
Those velvet ears – but pr'ythee do not stick
Thy latent talons in me . . .'

And who could doubt that **William Wordsworth** had watched *The Kitten and the Falling Leaves:*

'See the kitten on the wall
Sporting with the leaves that fall . . .
But the Kitten, how she starts,
Crouches, stretches, paws and darts!
First at one, and then its fellow:
. . . What intenseness of desire
In her upward eye of fire!

Edward Lear's work was inspired in part by a real cat, Foss, his companion of 17 years.

Lear's memorable cats included the Runcible cat with crimson whiskers who rowed round the world with a Quangle-Wangle, and the beautiful pussy in *The Owl and the Pussy-cat:*

'The Owl and the Pussy-cat went to sea
In a beautiful pea-green boat,
They took some honey, and plenty of money,
Wrapped up in a five-pound note.
The owl looked up to the stars above,
And sang to a small guitar,
'O lovely Pussy, O Pussy, my love,
What a beautiful Pussy you are,
You are

Edward Lear's seafaring owl and pussy-cat.

You are!
What a beautiful pussy you are!'

That Foss was the model for the Pussy-cat is indicated by Lear's drawings for the poem: the cat looks just like his drawings of Foss.

The cats in the 1885 edition of the early 19th-century doggerel poem *Dame Wiggin of Lee, and her Seven Wonderful Cats*, also had a familiar look to Victorian children, for they were drawn by one of the period's best-known artists, Kate Greenaway. The poem, very popular in its day, had a note on the title page of the first, 1823, edition that it had been 'written principally by a lady of ninety', later said to be a **Mrs Pearson** who had a toy shop in Fleet Street.

Among other things, Dame Wiggin's cats went to school, ate their food from a bowl with a spoon and

'When spring-time came back
They had breakfast of curds;
And were greatly afraid
Of disturbing the birds.
"If you sit, like good cats,
All sewn in a tree,
They will teach you to sing!"
Said Dame Wiggin of Lee.'

Christina Rossetti's cat, Grimalkin, died giving birth to a kitten. Mrs Rossetti told of her grief in *On the Death of a Cat: A Friend of Mine Aged Ten Years and a Half:*

'Who shall tell the lady's grief
When her Cat was past relief?
Who shall number the hot tears
Shed o'er her, belov'd for years?
Who shall say the dark dismay
Which her dying caused that day?'

Thomas Hardy, too, mourned the 'tragic end' of a 'companion torn away' in *Last Words to a Dumb Friend:*

'Pet was never mourned as you,
Purrer of the spotless hue,
Plumy tail, and wistful gaze
While you humoured our queer
ways,
Or outshrilled your morning call
up the stairs and through the
hall . . .'

T.S. Eliot's *Old Possum's Book of Practical Cats* was published in 1939, a last, light-hearted fling before war changed everything.

Eliot had had numerous cats of his own, and his poetic cats, who had developed out of years of telling cat poems to the children of friends, perhaps owed something of their style to them.

The cats in *Old Possum's Book of Practical Cats* are: the Old Gumbie Cat, whose name is ***Jennyanydots.*** 'She sits and sits and sits and sits – and that's what makes a Gumbie Cat!'; ***Growltiger***, a 'Bravo Cat, who travelled on a barge'; ***The Rum Tum Tugger***, who 'is a Curious Cat'; ***The Jellicle Cats***, who are sort-of ordinary cats, black and white, rather small, merry and bright, who develop slowly and are not too big; ***Mungojerrie*** and ***Rumpelteazer*** who 'were a very notorious couple of cats', a pair of 'knockabout clowns' living around Kensington; ***Old Deuteronomy***, a very old cat who has 'buried nine wives' and has a large progeny; the ***Great Rumpuscat***, who broke up and scattered a street fight between the Pekes and the Pollicles, while frightened neighbours could think of nothing better to do than ring up the Fire Brigade; ***Mr Mistoffelees***, 'The Original Conjuring Cat'; ***Macavity***: the Mystery Cat. 'He's outwardly respectable. (They say he cheats at cards,)' and whenever anything goes wrong or accidents happen, *'Macavity's not there!'*; ***Gus***, the theatre cat, whose name is really Asparagus; ***Bustopher Jones***: the Cat About Town – 'he's the St James's Street cat'; ***Skimbleshanks***: the Railway Cat who's in charge of the Night Mail; and ***Cat Morgan*** who 'once was a Pirate what sailed the 'igh seas', but who is now a commissionaire in Bloomsbury Square.

Don Marquis's Mehitable is another pre-World War II alley cat, though according to archy, the cockroach who writes about their lives (he's typing it all, but, being so small, can't manage the key shifts for punctuation or capital letters), she was cleopatra in an earlier life.

Archy and Mehitabel were created by Don Marquis and appeared regularly in two New York newspapers, the poems being collected and published in *Archy and Mehitabel* (1927) and *Archy's Life of Mehitabel* (1933). For many readers they provided an unforgettable portrait of the perfect alley cat, optimistic and insouciant, crying 'wotthehell, wotthehell' at the world and its problems and being 'toujours gai, toujours gai!'

Weighing Bulgy

To end this chapter on the cat and the English language, here is a piece of English journalism at its whimsical best.

The writer was William Connor, for many years known to millions of readers of the *Daily Mirror* as Cassandra.

Cassandra, as he had told his readers more than once, had a cat, 'the finest cat in Bucks south of a line drawn from Ludgershall to Wendover. . . . My cat can purr in his sleep, leap around the tree tops, pinch the best chair and eat more boiled fish or raw meat than any other living creature. He is insurpassable.'

But Cassandra had a problem with his cat, one which he finally solved while lying immobile in a hospital bed. On 5 January 1966, he told his *Daily Mirror* readers all.

'For years – nine in fact – I have been trying to weigh my splendid cat, Bulgy, on the bathroom scales. But could I do it? No sir. No sooner had I got the front legs on the platform than the back legs whipped off. I tried to force Bulgy down but the vertical pressure gave the wrong reading.

I tried holding him up like an undignified puss-in-boots and he fought like mad. I tried placing tempting fishy morsels on the scales hoping that he would climb aboard. No dice.

Then recently lying in my lonely bed in the small hours when good things of the day begin to droop and drowse while night's black agents to their preys do rouse (all royalties to W. Shakespeare), the solution flashed upon the inward eye which is the bliss of solitude (all royalties to W. Wordsworth).

Had I been in a bath and mobile, I would, like Archimedes, have leapt out yelling "Eureka!"

The moment I arrived home I grabbed Bulgy and leapt on to the bathroom scales.

Reading: 14 stones 2 pounds.

I let him go. I then remained on the scales.

Reading: 13 stones exactly. Net weight of the finest cat in the world: 16 pounds. Eureka!'

Cats in the Arts

Painted Cats

That cats are a popular subject with art lovers is indicated by the fact that of the London Tate Gallery's top ten or so best-selling postcards and greeting cards, reproducing works from the gallery's collections, three include cats:

The Graham Children by **William Hogarth** (1742), with its superb family pet enthusiatically eyeing an agitated goldfinch in a cage.

Cat, a sensitive and loving watercolour by **Gwen John** probably of one of her own pets, painted sometime between 1910 and 1920.

Mr and Mrs Clark and Percy by **David Hockney**, a large acrylic painting on canvas, painted

Cat *by Gwen John.*

1970–71, in which the splendidly elegant, white-furred Percy sits on Mr Ossie Clark's knee gazing out on to a balcony.

Here is a representative selection, of the artist's cat through history:

Cats depicted by the **Ancient Egyptians** include a lean and spotted animal, the Sun God Ra in cat form, on a papyrus 3,200 years old in *The Book of the Dead* and, on a wall painting from a tomb in Thebes, a cat taking part in a bird hunt.

A rare **Greek** depiction of a cat can be found on the base of a statue from *c.* 480 BC, if not earlier. The

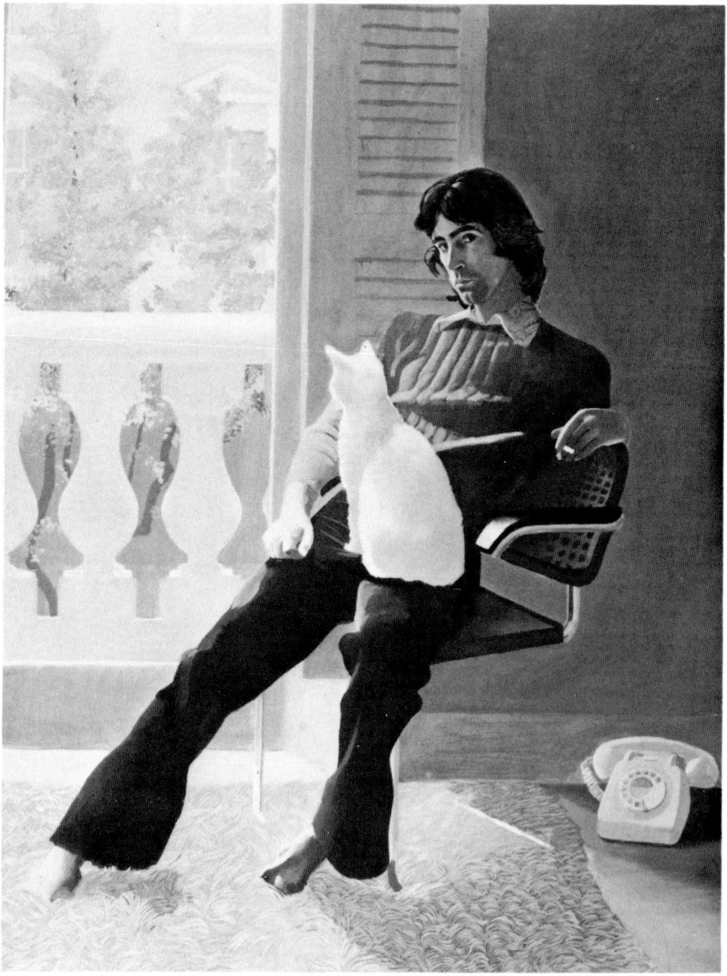

Detail from Mr. and Mrs. Clark and Percy *by David Hockney.*

scene includes some young men urging on a dog and a cat to fight each other. The cat is not well depicted; some observers reckon it is a weasel.

Cats were rarely included in early West European art, though it was given a place in the *Irish Book of Kells*, and it is not until we start looking at Italian Renaissance art that we see the cat being given any sort of prominence in paintings and drawings.

Leonardo da Vinci's page of drawings of cats is well known. Some of the cats are charming, the artist having deftly caught many typical poses, but others are very

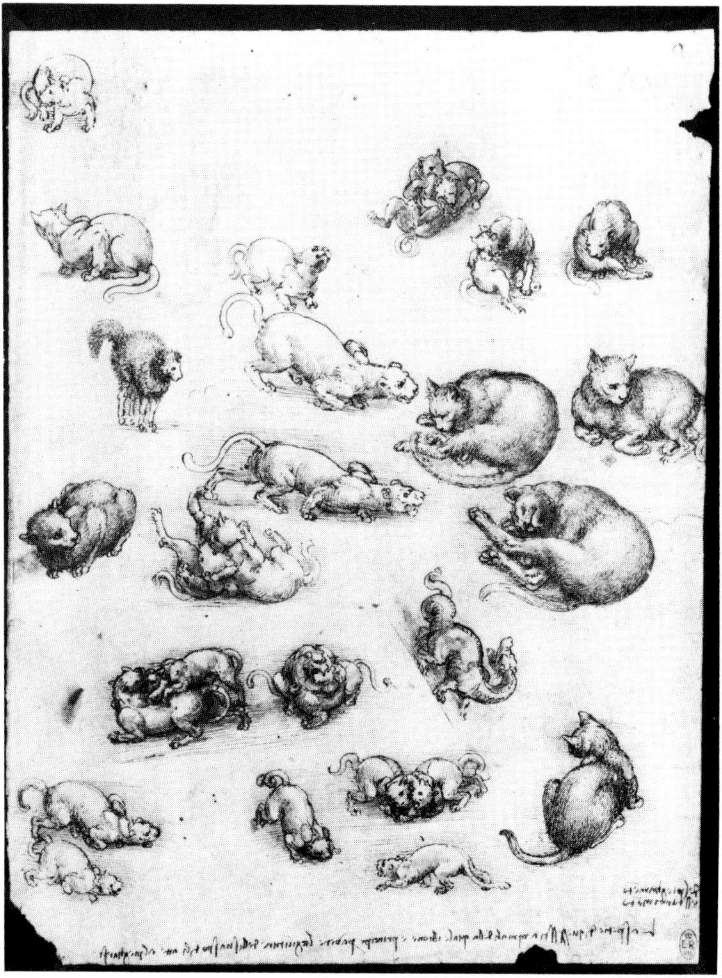

Cat studies by Leonardo da Vinci.

odd-looking indeed, as if Leonardo were trying to draw an animal combining the characteristics of the cat and of the funny little dragon who appears among them on the page.

The Venetian 16th-century painter, **Jacopo Bassano** included two fine white-and-tabby coloured cats in his *tour de force*, *Animals going into the Ark*, in the collection of Queen Elizabeth the Queen Mother.

A little boy plays with a pretty cat in the *Madonna del Gatto*, by another 16th-century Italian, **Federigo Baroccio**, in the National Gallery, London, which also has **Antonello da Messina**'s famous *St Jerome in His Study*, in which a delightful cat sits not far from the saint's feet.

Domenico Ghirlandaio sat a sad-looking cat next to Judas Iscariot in the foreground of his *Last Supper*, painted *c.* 1480 and now in the San Marco monastery in Florence. Over a century later, **Tintoretto** also included a cat in his *Last Supper*, in the Church of San Giorgio Maggiore in Venice. This cat, like the one in Tintoretto's *Annunciation* in the Stockholm Museum, is a less than pleasant-tempered animal and seems to be thinking distinctly wicked thoughts as it sits under a cloud. Perhaps, as critics have suggested, both Ghirlandaio's and Tintoretto's cats were meant to be seen as symbols of the Devil's presence at Christ's last meal.

Jan Breughel the Elder included a pretty blue-grey cat looking down on the stable from an upper window in his *Adoration of the Kings*, painted around 1598 (National Gallery, London).

The 17th-century artist, **Louis le Nain**, often put a neatly relaxed cat, perhaps sitting near the fire, in his paintings such as the *Peasant Family* (Louvre) and *The Dairywoman's Family* (Hermitage, Leningrad).

During the 18th century, **Francois Desportes** and **Jean Baptiste Chardin** created some very lively cats for their superb still-life paintings. Chardin's *La Raie* (The Skate, Louvre), in which the kitten stalking amongst the oyster shells is wonderfully life-like, is a particularly fine painting.

George Stubbs, one of the greatest of all painters of the horse, included a cat in his paintings of *The Godolphin Arabian*. This painting, done in the early 1790s some 40 years after the famous stallion had died, includes the cat less, it seems, as a portrait than as an illustration of a well-known anecdote. The cat had been a stablemate of the horse and is said to have kept vigil by its body, only leaving to slink off to a hayloft where it too, soon died. Stubbs did only one known study of a cat, *Miss Anne White's Kitten*.

A late 19th-century artist who devoted himself almost entirely to cats was the Franco-Swiss **Théophile Steinlen**. Working mainly in Paris, he produced thousands of cat pictures, most of them drawings based on his observations of the cats who stalked the alleys, gutters and rooftops of Montparnasse.

Edouard Manet, who drew many fine cats put a small black cat at the feet of the splendid *Olympia* when he painted her in 1863. The little cat, self-contained and serene, is

Miss Anne White's Kitten *the only surviving study of a cat by George Stubbs, dated 1790.*

more of a sketch than a full-blooded portrait. Manet was not approaching his cat with the same artistic fervour as **Gericault** and **Delacroix** had done before him. There are numerous cat studies by these two French artists which must stand alongside the very best cats in art.

Manet's friend, **Auguste Renoir**, had more of an affinity with cats. Those he included in *Madame Julie Manet* and *Girl with a Cat* (Metropolitan Museum, New York) are playful and lively, with much

the same voluptuous, sensual look that Renoir gave to the women in his paintings.

Henri Rousseau, who, like Delacroix, could paint a superb big cat, could also paint a small domestic cat with style. There is a neat little black cat chasing a ball of wool in Rousseau's *Portrait of a Woman* in the Jeu de Paume in Paris.

English artist **Gwen John** spent most of her working life in France where she lived quietly, accompanied more often than not by several cats of whom she made many fine studies which today fetch comparatively high prices at auction. After her death at Dieppe in 1939, her brother, Augustus John, reported back to a friend that 'She had brought no baggage whatever, but as it turned out had not forgotten to make in her will a suitable provision for the cats.'

Girl with a Cat *by Auguste Renoir.*

Performing cats

Cats will perform only when they want to, not when asked to do so by others, and on a live television programme such independence can have unfortunate results. Cats have done better on film, where they can be rehearsed and filmed in short snatches, and have had starring roles in numerous movies as well as providing lively motifs in the opening credits of many more. And in television advertising, cats have proved great salesmen.

Arthur, a splendidly built white British shorthair was, for a decade, the most famous cat in Britain. His particular skill was to use his left paw to scoop catfood out of a tin, and then eat it with obvious enjoyment. Initially, Arthur was hired by pet-food manufacturers, Spillers, to use on the wrapper of the Kattomeat tins. Then they bought him for £1,000 and used him in a series of commercials which cost them a well-spent £3 million. Arthur was asked to work only about nine days a year but still made more than 30 commercials between 1966 and 1975. His television 'voice' was provided by actors as famous as Peter Bull, Leo McKern and Joss Ackland. Arthur died in February 1976, a month short of his 17th birthday.

Such was the selling power of Arthur's eating paw that a decade after his death Spillers decided to find another Arthur to promote their Kattomeat. They called in animal trainer Ann Head and she found the perfect replacement in an animal shelter. While not naturally addicted to eating with his paw, Arthur II proved an apt pupil and one, moreover, happy to

Arthur II taking a dip!

scoop up Kattomeat in a film studio full of bright lights and film crew. The new Arthur, a fine, green-eyed, white shorthair, first appeared on British commercial television in January 1987, when he was 2 years old. All the signs were that he would have a long and happy career as a telly star.

Other white cats who have had an honourable place in British advertising have been the chinchillas who have helped advertise Kosset Carpets for more than 20 years. Star of the advertisement for the past ten years has been Jemari Michaelsson. Solomon was another superb chinchilla who advertised carpets, but he went on to even greater things, becoming a movie star with roles in *Diamonds Are Forever* and *A Clockwork Orange*.

Arthur's equivalent in the United States of America was Morris, whose stylish endorsements of 9 Lives cat food made him the country's No. 1 cat celebrity. He won an award as the best animal actor in TV commercials in 1973 and, like Arthur, had his biography published. When Morris died in 1978, a long search for his successor resulted in Morris II, found in a cat home, and now just as famous as his predecessor. As well as working about 20 days a year to film his TV commercials, Morris II flies first class all over the United States in support of adopt-a-pet schemes.

In Japan television, magazine and billboard advertisers have been queuing up to hire Mr Satoru Tsadu's cats, a troupe of patiently trained cats who perform a number of tricks in fancy dress. Recently Mr Tsadu's cats, themselves living in the lap of luxury, were said to be earning their owner a million dollars a month.

Back in the 19th century an Italian showman called Pietro Capelli won an international reputation with his circus-style cats. They could balance on the high wire, do a trapeze act and juggle with their hind legs. They apparently needed very few commands from Signor Capelli, who spoke to them in three languages.

Mr Hafizoali was a more modest performer on an American radio station in the 1950s. For many years the sound of Mr Hafizoali's purr, sent out over the airwaves every morning at 8 o'clock, got the listeners to Radio WJZ off to a good start.

A feline performer who amused viewers of California's Channel 7 television station in the late 1970s was Dudley, owned by Mrs Jeanne Wood of California. Before he hurt his hip, Dudley would do up to 30 tricks when commanded, including shaking hands, playing checkers, typing, and rolling over when asked.

Frazier, a shaded silver Persian from Houston, Texas, could play the piano, so his owner averred, and reached the finals of the All-American Glamour Kitz Contest, sponsored by Kitz Pan Litter, in 1974.

In Potter's Museum of Curiosities in Arundel, Sussex, kittens perform for visitors every day the museum is open. The cats, all of whom are Victorian, are among the collection of stuffed animals and natural curiosities made by Victorian taxidermist, Walter Potter, who first began exhibiting the results of his considerable skill in 1861. Among such carefully constructed scenes as *The Guinea Pigs' Cricket Match* and *The House That Jack Built*, are two scenes involving kittens. *The Kittens' Tea and Croquet Party* includes 37 kittens, sitting round a tea table, playing croquet or riding a bicycle; *The Kittens' Wedding* has a bride, six bridesmaids, a groom, a parson and numerous guests. The museum is careful to tell its visitors that the kittens were not killed just to make an exhibit in a museum.

Fittleworth was the ninth cat to join the cast of the original London production of Bill Naughton's comedy *Spring and Port Wine*, which opened at the Mermaid Theatre in November 1965. When the play transferred to the New Theatre (now the Albery) in 1967, Fittleworth went too, having lasted longer in the role, which involved eating a herring on stage, than any of his predecessors.

OPERATIC CATS

Cats have ben thought worthy of a

place in the world of opera, too. Maurice Ravel introduced some splendid caterwauling for baritone and mezzo-soprano into his one-cat opera *L'Enfant et Les Sortilèges* (1925) in the form of a very realistic cat duet, the 'miaows' for which were supplied by Colette, who wrote the libretto for the opera in eight days.

Her story concerned a small boy whose teatime tantrum was punished then forgiven by the objects and animals around him: a cup and teapot, a book, an aviary and cats, frogs, squirrels, owls and dragonflies.

More recently, German composer Hanz Werner Henze has written an entire 'cat' opera, *The English Cat*, first performed in Santa Fe in 1983, and was broadcast on radio in London in 1986.

The opera, based on a story by Balzac and with a libretto by English playwright Edward Bond, is set in Victorian London. In true opera tradition, the hero, a handsome tomcat called Tom and heroine, innocent country cat, Minette, meet sad ends by the time the opera is over, but the general tone of the opera is light and satirical, with the cats clearly intended as caricatures of human foibles and failings.

Cartoon cats

ON SCREEN . . .

The first cartoon cat was a cheeky black mog called Krazy Kat. He began life in America in 1910 as a Hearst newspapers strip character, drawn by George Herriman. Krazy Kat's move to the silent screen came in 1916, via another Hearst outfit, International Film Service, which starred him with a mouse (a pointer to the future of the cartoon cat!) in *Krazy Kat and Ignatz Mouse*. Since Herriman was more interested in using Krazy Kat to express ideas rather than in giving him a distinctive character, Krazy Kat cartoons never had enormous appeal. Even so, his career lasted well into the 1930s, two of his later cartoons being *Krazy's Newsreel* (1936) and *Krazy's Magic* (1939).

The first cat movie super star was Felix the Cat. In his heyday in the 1920s Felix, who had a truly individual personality which movie audiences responded to, was more popular even than Charlie Chaplin, Buster Keaton or Harold Lloyd. His theme song, 'Felix kept on Walking', sold as sheet music by the million and was whistled and sung wherever movies were shown; cat food named after him sold by the ton (and still does in the UK); and Felix comic books and comic strips, and other ephemera, were lapped up by his devoted fans. Felix first appeared on the screen

in 1922; his creators, Australian-born Pat Sullivan and artist Otto Messmer, made a short film called *Feline Follies* which was added to a Pathe screen magazine short. By 1928 about 80 Felix films had been made, with Sullivan and Messmer producing their last Felix film, *The Last Life*, in 1929. Felix lived on, however, in the hands of other film makers, with Burt Gillet producing the first Felix colour film, *Felix the Cat and the Goose that Laid the Golden Egg*, in 1936. In the 1960s a Felix TV series was produced.

The greatest cat and mouse duo in cartoon films has to be the seven Oscar-winning partnership of Tom and Jerry. Tom was the cat, an obvious alley cat in a comfortable house complete with delightful black housekeeper, and Jerry was the scared-of-nobody, quick-thinking mouse. The two were created for Metro-Goldwyn-Mayer by William Hanna and Joseph Barbera. These two had a big success in 1937 with a cartoon called *Puss Gets the Boot*, starring Jasper the Cat and an un-named mouse. The cartoon was nominated for an Academy Award, and Hanna and Barbera decided to continue the formula. By the time their next cartoon, *The Midnight Snack*, was completed, the cat and mouse had become Tom and Jerry. Apart from their many cartoons, Tom and Jerry also appeared in two live-action films, Jerry dancing with Gene Kelly in *Anchors Aweigh* (1945) and both of them swimming with Esther Williams in *Dangerous When Wet* (1953). Their CinemaScope debut came in 1954 in the cartoon *Pet Peeves*. In all, Tom and Jerry appeared in 154 shorts, and their antics are still delighting children and adults alike on television and video film.

The seven Tom and Jerry cartoons by Hanna and Barbera and producer Fred Quimby to win Oscars were: *Yankee Doodle Mouse* (1943), *Mouse Trouble* (1944), *Quiet Please* (1945), *The Cat Concerto* (1946), *The Little Orphan* (1948), *Two Mousketeers* (1951) and *Johann Mouse* (1952).

Other cat-and-mouse duos were Little Roquefort (the mouse) and Percy (the cat), around whom numerous cartoons were made in the 1940s, and Herman and Katnip appearing first in *Naughty but Nice* in 1947, with a series of cartoons following. Neither pair posed a serious threat to Tom and Jerry's supremacy.

The cat who never got the bird was that rough, tough, bad ol' puddy tat Sylvester, who had such trouble saying his 's's in a series of cartoons made by Fritz Frelang for Warner Brothers. In fact, Tweetie Pie, the tiny canary Sylvester never quite caught, appeared first, in a cartoon called *Birdie and Beast* (1944). Sylvester followed with *Kitty Kornered* (1945). Then, Tweetie Pie cried 'I taut I taw a puddy tat!' and the pair were launched on an enormously popular series of cartoons which lasted 15 years. The man responsible for their voices, Mel Blanc, even made a record of the two, and there was an Oscar, in 1947, for *Tweetie Pie*. Sylvester also appeared in cartoons with other characters, including his son, Sylvester Jr, Speedy Gonzales and Porky Pig.

A short-lived British pair was Chester the Cat and Felia. They

were part of the family of characters created for J. Arthur Rank's short-lived foray into film cartoon production after World War II. In 1945 Rank set up a company, Gaumont British Animation, which worked from a studio in the tiny riverside town of Cookham. The results were never very exciting and cartoon production trickled out in the 1950s.

The lady cat with the great voice, provided by Judy Garland, was Mewsette, the leading lady in a feature-length cartoon of the early sixties, *Gay Purree*. Mewsette was a lovely French lady cat lured to Paris by the city's bright lights, only to fall foul of a band of villains, one of whom, Madame Rubens Chatte, spoke with the voice of Hermione Gingold.

Walt Disney's best cats. Although Walt Disney created a couple of cat characters in his very early films, cats had no part in the Disney stock company as it evolved after the debut of Mickey Mouse in 1928. It was not until 1970 that the Disney genius took feline form. The film was the 78mm feature-length cartoon, *The Artistocats*, which featured Thomas O'Malley, a good-hearted drifter from the alley, whose part was spoken and sung by Phil Harris, and Thomas' gorgeous lady love, Duchess, given a voice by Eva Gabor. Duchess's artistokittens were called Marie, Toulouse and Berlioz.

The most successful television star is probably Top Cat. Created in 1961 by the famous Hollywood cartoon production studio of Hanna-Barbera (producers for 18 years of the Tom and Jerry cartoons for MGM), Top Cat is a laid-back, streetwise animal of dubious morals and probably mildly criminal antecedents. Very popular with children, his cool approach to life among the garbage cans also appeals to adults.

The first animated feature film to be given an X certificate was *Fritz the Cat*, created by underground cartoonist Robert Crumb in the magazine *Comix*, and put on to the cinema screen by Ralph Bakshi in 1972. The film's coarseness and crudity and its explicit sexuality set a precedent for animated film makers, and spawned a sequal, *The Nine Lives of Fritz the Cat* (1974).

Top Cat – feline cunning and charm at its best.

ON PAPER . . .

The first comic cartoon cats for children were the 'Rainbow Cats' Colony,' a lively bunch of Louis Wain-like cats who appeared in *Rainbow*, the first British comic to be aimed at the child reader. *Rainbow* was first published in 1914, used colour printing, and lasted up to the 1950s.

The best-selling cartoon cat is probably that irrepressible, disreputable, fat cat, Garfield. Unleashed upon a delighted world from the clever pen of American cartoonist Jim Davis in 1978, by 1982 Garfield was appearing in comic strip form in not far short of a thousand newspapers. By this time, three Garfield books, *Garfield Bigger than Life, Garfield Gains Weight*, and *Garfield at Large*, had appeared at the same time on the *New York Times* trade paperbacks bestseller list, something never achieved before by any author. The total sales figures for these three books is well over two million copies. Since then, Garfield has appeared in many more books and on television and video films, and has branched out into a huge, world-wide spin-off industry which has put his face, figure and many of his choicest remarks on items ranging from children's pencil sets to women's panties.

Runner-up is another American, Bernard Kliban. His best-selling book of cat drawings, *Cat*, was published in 1975 and within six years had reprinted 25 times, selling more than a million copies in the United States alone. The Kliban cat, typically a strongly striped and round-eyed animal, has been described by his creator as 'One hell of a nice animal, frequently mistaken for a meatloaf.'

The most tasteless cartoon book must be Simon Bond's *101 Uses for a Dead Cat* which sold over a million copies in the UK, US and elsewhere in 1981–2, the year of publication.

Three great post-war cartoonists who have caricatured the cat brilliantly have been the American artist Saul Steinberg, Frenchman Siné with his witty series of cats illustrating 'cat' words such as catalogue and catastrophe, and Englishman Ronald Searle, whose first book of cat cartoons, *Searle's Cats* (Dobson Books, 1967) also appeared in American, Canadian, French, German and Japanese editions. Searle's follow-ups, *More Cats* (Dobson, 1975) and Searle's *Big Fat Cat Book* (Macmillan 1982) also found large sales abroad, and the cats in them have found their way on to other merchanise, such as mugs, postcards and greetings cards.

The cat at the movies

Unlike dogs, who have been successful screen heroes from the earliest days of the moving picture, cats have all too seldom been given major roles in the cinema (except in cartoon form, as we have noted earlier in this chapter). On the whole, cats have been bit players in the movies, though often very effective ones.

In *La Dolce Vita* (Italy 60) there was a kitten providing its own innocent commentary on the decadence portrayed so vividly by Federico Fellini.

In *Breakfast at Tiffany's* (US 61)

You Only Live Twice, *starring Sean Connery, Donald Pleasence and Solomon!*

there was a beautiful pet, called simply Cat, whose presence was so important to Holly Golightly (Audrey Hepburn).

Strolling through the title credits of *Walk on the Wild Side* (US 62) was a cat, hinting at the steamy tale of life in New Orleans to come.

In two James Bond films the chief villain of the tale, Bloefeld – Donald Pleasence in *You Only Live Twice* (GB 67) and Charles Gray in *Diamonds are Forever* (GB 71) – each had a superb white Chinchilla (real name Solomon) which they caressed in sinister fashion at high points in the drama.

The horror movie genre has exploited the idea of the cat's mysterious nature, producing numerous tales of people who have turned into cats or disguised themselves as cats for various chilling reasons.

The play *The Cat and The Canary* has been made into a movie several times. The first, silent, version included a truly terrifying cat figure, with claws clutching at the throat of heroine Laura La Plante. The first sound version of the play was called *The Cat Creeps* (US 30), with Neil Hamilton creeping about in cloak and cat-like claws. Then came the splendid 1939 version, *The Cat and the Canary*, with Bob Hope and Paulette Goddard being threatened by a murderous villain heavily disguised in cat mask and with hairy, long-clawed hands.

Cat People (US 42) was a successful B movie made by Val Lewton in which the horror was cleverly kept off-screen so that audiences did not actually see Simone Simon suffer the family curse and turn into a black panther.

The Curse of the Cat People (US 44) A sequel to *Cat People.*

The Catman of Paris (US 46) Robert Wilkes hides behind cat whiskers.

Cat Women of the Moon (US 54) An early look at the possibilities of felines in space, this time centred on a tribe of telepathic cat-like women.

The Cat Creeps (US 46) Cats prowl about amongst a group of people threatened by Egyptian curses and some suspected reincarnation.

Cat Girl (GB 58) A beautiful girl begins to show disastrous feline characteristics.

Apart from all this horror, the cat has been allowed to be more or less itself in several movies, appearing not as a bit player, but as a character with a role essential to the story line:

The Black Cat (US 41) Based on the famous Edgar Allan Poe story, is a comedy thriller about the scheming relatives of an eccentric, cat-loving old lady, waiting for her to die so that they can inherit her wealth. One of the relatives speeds up the happy day by murdering her, but when the will is read out they discover that no-one can inherit until the last of her many cats has died.

Rhubarb (US 51) A comedy about an alley cat called Rhubarb who, inheriting a fortune and a major league baseball team from his millionaire owner, becomes the mascot who leads the team to a pennant.

The Shadow of the Cat (GB 61) Another tale of murder and mayhem, in which the cat owned by the murder victim apparently causes the deaths of relatives searching for the woman's will.

Puss-in-Boots (Mexico 61) A Mexican version of the famous fairy tale.

One Day, A Cat (Czechoslovakia 63) A delightful fantasy about a cat who wears glasses and the effect he has on local villagers when he takes them off.

Three Lives of Thomasina (US/GB 63) A children's fairy tale based on Paul Gallico's novel, *Thomasina, the Cat who Thought she was God.*

Mexican cartoon version of Puss-in-Boots.

Thomasina becomes the heroine of this Disney movie about a little girl (Karen Dotrice) who loses all joy in life when her cat has to be put to sleep, and who seeks out a mysterious healer to bring the cat back to her . . .

Under the Yum Yum Tree (US 63) Has an acrobatic feline following amorous landlord Jack Lemmon around as he attempts to seduce his lovely tenant, Carol Lynley.

The Incredible Journey (Canada 63) This Disney movie about a Siamese cat and two dogs, separated from their owner, who cross hundreds of miles of rugged terrain in Canada to return home, was based on the story by Sheila Burnford.

That Darn Cat (US 65) Another Disney film, in which the Siamese cat hero helps the FBI, Dean Jones and Hayley Mills, solve a case.

Cat! (US 66) A movie for kids about a boy who befriends a wildcat which later saves him from a deadly peril.

Eye of the Cat (US 69) Michael Sarazin, despite suffering from ailurophobia, tries to do away with his wealthy, cat-loving aunt (Eleanor Parker), but reckons without her protective moggies, a horde of which finally do the scheming nephew to death.

The Night of the Thousand Cats (Mexico 72) Horror again, this time about a demented aristocrat (Hugo Stiglitz) who keeps a thousand man-eating cats in his castle feeding them on the flesh of attractive young ladies.

Harry and Tonto (US 74) Art Carney gave an Oscar-winning performance as Harry, an elderly New York widower who, when evicted from his apartment, decides to make one last great trip across America, taking his cat, Tonto, with him, to start a new life in California.

I Am a Cat (Japan 75) A look at the life of a teacher and his family in early 20th-century Japan through the eyes of a cat.

The Cat From Outer Space (US 78) Another Disney fantasy, about a spaceship commanded by a cat called Jake, whose collar gives him amazing powers – which he needs when his spaceship has to make an emergency landing on earth.

Our Johnny (Austria 80) A look at the influence a cat can have on a family, telling the story of a cat called Johnny who considerably disrupts the smooth tenor of a life in an ordinary household.

Cat's Eye (US 85) Three slight stories by Stephen King, linked by a wandering cat.

The Black Cat (Italy 85) A recent,

Rhubarb made his acting debut as a baseball team owner and won a PATSY award.

Cat savouring his award-winning performance in Breakfast At Tiffany's.

but probably not the last, movie to deal with the mysterious powers of cats. This time the film centred on Patrick Magee, an investigator into the paranormal, whose cat is suspected of causing some mysterious deaths in an English village.

THE PATSY AWARDS

In 1951 The American Humane Association started a Picture Animal Top Star of the Year (PATSY) award scheme and in 1958 extended it to include television performers and other categories. Among the many animals to receive Patsy awards, including a seal, a goose, a wolf, a rat, a red deer and a bull, there has been a number of cats.

1952 First Place: Rhubarb, for film *Rhubarb.*

1959 First Place: Pyewacket, for film *Bell, Book and Candle.*

1962 First Place: Cat, for film *Breakfast at Tiffany's.*

1966 First Place: Syn Cat, for film *That Darn Cat.*

1973 Special Commercial Award: Morris, for Nine Lives Cat Food.

1974 Television Series: Midnight, for *Mannix* series.

1975 Motion Pictures: Tonto, for film *Harry and Tonto.*

1977 Special Award: 17, for *Dr. Shrinker.*

1978 Special Award: Amber, for film *The Cat From Outer Space.*

Awards all round for Art Carney and friend in Harry and Tonto.

Amber, in her award-winning role as The Cat From Outer Space.

1986 Special Category: The cats, for *Alfred Hitchcock Presents* television series.

Mail cats

A recent philatelic publication reckoned that 115 countries have put 750 cats, great and small, on stamps since the mid-1950s. In the past four years, complete series of domestic cat stamps have been issued by Korea (1983), Nicaragua (1984), Guinea, Guinea-Bissau and Kampuchea (all 1985). Domestic cats which have appeared on stamps include:

Abyssinian
Bulgaria, 1967
3 stotinki; head of adult cat.
Guinea, 1985
35 sily; head of adult cat.

Angora
Bulgaria, 1967
1 stotinki; kitten.
Hungary, 1968
60 fillers; cream angora
1 forint 50; white
2 forints; striped
5 forints; blue.

Burmese
Mongolia, 1978
1 kyat; adult cat.
Nicaragua, 1984
4 cordoba; head of blue adult.

Chinchilla
Philippines, 1979
Cats and Dogs series, 5 pesos; adult cat.
Nicaragua, 1984
Red 50 centavos; head of adult.

Domestic non-pedigree
Luxembourg, 1961
Animal Protection series, 150 francs; tabby.
Ascension Islands, 1983
Introduced Species series, 20 pence; adult tabby.
Poland, 1964
30 groszy: head of black cat

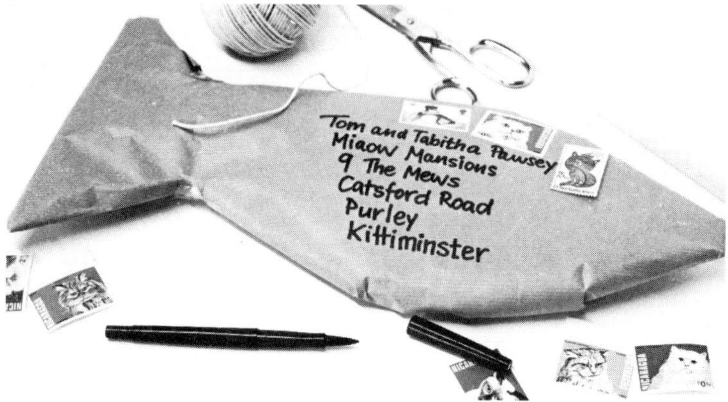

Cats are a popular subject for thematic stamp collections.

40 groszy: head of grey kitten
1 zloty 55: grey striped kitten
2 zloty 50: tiger-striped cat.
Albania, 1966
15 qintars: tabby adult.
Mongolia, 1978
Domestic Cats series, 10 mongo: silver tabby.
Philippines, 1979
Cats and Dogs series, 90 centavos; striped tabby.

Manx
Isle of Man, 1973
10 pence: adult.

Marmalade/red colour
Poland, 1964
60 groszy: yellow and white non-pedigree.
Romania, 1965
10 bani: ginger tabby tom.
Nicaragua, 1984
1 cordoba; red tabby longhair.

Persian
Poland, 1964
90 groszy; head of a white Persian
1 zloty 35; head of an orange Persian
3 zloty 40; blue Persian.
Romania, 1965
40 bani; 2 white Persians.
Yeman, 1965
⅛ fils; head of a black Persian
1 fils; silver tabby Persian
2 fils; cream tabby Persian.
Nicaragua, 1984
Blue 50 centavos; white Persian.

Siamese
Poland, 1964
50 groszy; Seal Point adult.
Romania, 1965
1 leu 35; Seal Point adult.
Albania, 1966
10 quintars: Seal Point adult.
Thailand, 1971
Siamese series: Seal Point, Chocolate Point, Blue Point and White (recognized in the UK as an Oriental Short-hair).
Nicaragua, 1984
3 cordobas; head of Chocolate Point adult.
Guinea, 1985
7 syli; Lilac Point adult.
Kampuchea, 1985
Domestic Cats series, 1 riel: Chocolate Point adult.

Tortoiseshell
Yemen, 1965
¼ fils; adult.

Nicaragua, 1984
2 cordobas; head of adult.

Cats from art
Yugoslavia, 1965
Children's Week series, 30 dinar; 'lucky black cat', cartoon-style.
East Germany, 1967
International Children's Day
5 pfennigs: cartoon-style 'He-cat'.
East Germany, 1972
Children's television characters, 5 pfennigs: 'Mauz and Hoppel' (a cat and a hare).
Japan, 1979
Modern Japanese Art set, 50 yen: black cat by a tree, by Shunso Hishida.

Cats from folklore, etc.
Hungary, 1960
Fairy Tales (2nd series), 60 fillers: Puss-in-Boots.
Poland, 1968
Fairy Tales series, 20 groszy: Puss-in-Boots.
United Kingdon, 1985
Christmas series, 34 pence; pantomime cat.

Cats and people
Netherlands, 1952
Children's Welfare set, 5 cents and 10 cents: boy with a cat.
New Zealand, 1974
Health Stamps, 1 cent and 3 cents: drawings of children with a cat and dog.
Cuba, 1957
50th Anniversary of the Jeanette Ryder Foundation (for animals welfare), 4 centavos: Jeanette Ryder with 2 dogs and a cat.

The cat's ancestors
North Korea, 1964
5 chon sepia; European Wild Cat.
Czechoslovakia, 1967
Fauna of Tatra National Park series, 60 halers black and buff; European Wild Cat
North Korea, 1974
15th Anniversary Pyongyong Zoo, 2 chon; European Wild Cat.
United Kingdon, 1986
Nature Conservation series, 31 pence; Wild Cat (*Felis Silvestris*).
Guinea, 1985
Domestic Cats series, 25 syli: European Wild Cat.

POSTCARD CATS
Postcards, which could be sent through the post without an envelope or cover, were introduced in Britain in 1870, and within a very short time had become enormously popular. Cat designs, or 'catland' postcards as they are called by collectors and enthusiasts, outnumbered all other animals on postcards put together.

Louis Wain is the most famous of all 'catland' postcard artists, his round-eyed, amusing, slightly mad-looking moggies being instantly recognisable. Towards the end of his life, when Wain had virtually succumbed to the schizophrenia which had long dogged him, his cats became extraordinary creatures indeed, but in his heyday, Wain's cats were cartoon creatures, with distinctly human characteristics and doing human activities. Wain began his career as a magazine and book illustrator, with cats appearing more and more often in his work from about 1890 (by which time he had acquired cats of his own). His first postcards, which appeared in 1902, were made from the illustration plates of books he had done for the well-known book and postcard publisher Raphael Tuck. Thereafter, Wain's cat postcard production was large and varied, reflecting his own great interest in

Three scenes from A Kitten's Christmas Party *by Louis Wain:*
1 Kittens writing the invitations.
2 At the ball
3 And so to bed.

cats; he had been elected President of the National Cat Club in 1890, in succession to Harrison Weir, the club's founder.

Violet Roberts specialised in amusingly drawn 'glamour' cats – cats with huge bows, lady cats with huge, Ascot-style hats – and, during World War I, cats expressing patriotism in every whisker. She produced two series of Regimental Cats and two called 'Khaki and Fluff' during the war.

William Henry Ellman used his cats to illustrate some of the great social phenomena of the day, such as the glamorous Gibson Girl and the less glamorous Suffragette, or slightly naughty themes such as mixed bathing at the seaside. He also turned to more patriotic themes during the war, drawing cats in typical 'Tommy Atkins' uniform and situations (he called his cats 'Tommy C-Atkins).

Tom Brown, a professional artist and founder of the London Sketch Club, also drew about a dozen humorous and stylish cat cards for the postcard publishers, Davidson Brothers, in the Edwardian period.

Arthur Thiele (1841–1919) was a German artist whose postcards, produced in abundance, sold widely in Britain. His fully-dressed cats indulging in all sorts of human activities were caricatures rather than cartoons, and the liveliness of his drawings made his cards very popular. His output, from about 1900 to just after the end of World War I, was among the largest of the period.

Helena Maguire (1860–1909), the daughter of an artist, was well-known for her chocolate box cats and kittens, though her postcards provided some very charming and pretty cats for Edwardian card fanciers. Cats were included in the

A 'catland' postcard by Helena Maguire.

Animal Studies series she did for Raphael Tuck, and she was also published by the German publisher, Hildesheimer and Co.

Maurice Boulanger, a French artist, was another 'cat' man whose postcards sold well in Britain.

Other late Victorian and Edwardian 'catland' artists from Britain whose work still sells among collectors include **G.L. Barnes**, who drew cats for the Tuck 'Oilette' range, **Arthur Butcher**, **Dorothy Travers Pope**, **Reg Carter**, **B. Cobbe**, **A.E. Kennedy** and **A.F. aydon.**

Heraldic Cats

In all the centuries of heraldic art, cats have made relatively few appearances, giving place in the main to their more noble cousins, lions and leopards.

The **Romans** used the cat on ensigns and banners, probably in allusion to the concept of liberty, since the Roman goddess of Liberty was generally depicted with a cat at her feet. Historians say that the first heraldic cats were probably those which appeared on the arms of at least three Roman legions or companies. One, the *Felices seniores*, adopted a red cat, and another a green striped one.

A wild cat was an emblem of the great **house of Burgundy** around the 5th century AD, and Clotilde of Burgundy, wife of Clovis, King of the Franks, is known to have carried as her emblem a sable cat killing a rat on a gold ground.

Since the **medieval Church** felt considerable hostility towards the cat, it is not surprising that few cats appeared in armorial bearings of this period. Some may even have been quietly turned into greater

The crest of J.R.B. Dawson Esq. of Runcorn, Cheshire.

beasts: it is thought that the three leopards which supported the Royal Arms of Great Britain, and which came via William the Conqueror and the Normans in 1066, were originally cats.

The **Dutch** republic adopted the cat as its emblem because of the animal's association with the concept of liberty.

The First **French** Republic added a cat to its emblem, in obvious reference to the Roman Republic.

Several **English** families included the cat in their badges or crests, including the Catesby family, which chose a spotted cat, and the Dawsons, whose cat was a tabby with a rat in its jaws.

The cat-a-mountain has been an emblem for several English and Scottish families. In **Scotland**, the adoption of the cat as a badge derived from the old far north province of Cat, which took its name from its Teutonic settlers, the Catti. 'Caithness' is the modern form of the name. The crest of the Mackintosh clan is a 'cat-a-mountain salient guardant proper', its supporters being 'two cats proper', and several other clans also have the cat-a-mountain in their crests.

Among **English peerages** to have included cats-a-mountain in their arms was that of the barons Muncaster, the title of the Pennington family of Muncaster, Co. Cumberland, whose crest included 'a mountain cat passant guardant proper'; and that of the famous Anglo-Norman family of de Burgh, one of whose descendants became Marquess of Clanricarde in 1825. One of his crests included a 'cat-a-mountain sejant guardant proper, collared and chained or', and the supporters of the coat of arms were 'two cats-a-mountain guardant proper, collared and chained or'. Both these peerages are extinct.

Cult of the Cat

Throughout religious history the cat has figured in dual roles, as symbols both of good and evil, as light and darkness, as the sun and moon, as the true religion and black magic. The late medieval Christian church took against the cat. Flying in the face of Jesus Christ himself who had, according to the Apocrypha gospels, counselled tenderness towards the cat, medieval Christians saw in the cat an emissary of the devil. Its connection with witches at a time when the church saw in witchcraft a threat to the church and to society, made the cat guilty too and in many parts of Roman Catholic Europe it became an object of paranoic horror and hate. With the rise of Protestantism, the cat became an anti-papacy symbol as well. In contrast, the cat has been worshipped, or been a focus for veneration, in several religions.

The sacred cat

Egypt

The cat achieved its greatest honour in Ancient Egypt. The Egyptians gave several of their most important gods cat shapes, or the heads of cats. The Sun god, Ra, most important of the gods of Egypt, was depicted as a cat as early as 3,000 years ago. The cat's

The great goddess of Ancient Egypt, Bast, with four kittens at her feet.

independent, night-stalking nature ensured its connection with the great goddess Bast, representative of the moon, which was seen as the Sun god's eye during the hours of darkness; the eyes of the cat were said to mirror the Sun's rays during the hours that the Sun itself was outside man's sight. Also known as Bubastis and Pasht, and the second member of the trio of gods of ancient Memphis, Bast was often represented with the head of a cat. Her cult centre was Bubastis on the Lower Nile, where the Jews lived for centuries, and she was worshipped from around 2,000 BC, her temple cats being carefully tended in special courts, and still had followers when the Roman Emperor Theodosias suppressed paganism in Egypt in AD 392.

The second goddess linked with the Sun god Ra, Sekhmet, was also often depicted as cat-headed, though she was also given the head of a lioness.

The Egyptians believed that the female cat brought forth 28 young – first one, then two, then three kittens and so on until she had given birth to seven kittens in one litter, the total of 28 representing the different degrees of light which shone from the moon during its waxing and waning.

The cat was so sacred in Egypt that anyone killing a cat was himself sentenced to death; when a household cat died, the occupants of the house shaved off their eyebrows in mourning and performed complicated funeral rites, including burying the embalmed body of the cat in special cat necropolises.

The Romans
The practical Romans recognized the value of the cat as a pet and a protector from mice and rats, but they also adopted it as a religious symbol, taking over from the Egyptians the cats' connections with the great moon goddess, Artemis, or Diana, Queen of Heaven. The Goddess was often depicted with a cat at her feet, a symbol of liberty.

Northern Europe
The pagan Teutonic goddess of Love and Beauty, Freya, was said to have a chariot drawn by two cats, and her cult included the honouring of cats. They were considered appropriate animals for the goddess because of their fecundity and their 'domestic' rather than wild nature. A cat-headed god was also found in pagan Ireland.

South America
In Peru, the Mohics worshipped a male deity, Ai Apaec, the god of copulation, in the form of a cat. The cat also appeared in the religions of the Incas and the Aztecs in Mexico.

South-east Asia
Both Thailand (Siam) and Burma had their own breeds of temple cats, the Siamese and the Birman, venerated as guardians of the countries' Buddhist temple. Once, the peoples of Thailand and Burma jealously guarded their sacred cats. Now, of course, Siamese and Birmans are particularly sought after in the West. The Siamese cat first came to Britain in the 1870s and the Birman to France in 1919, where it was sent to a British army officer who had helped Burmese priests during World War I.

Both the Thai people and the

Burmese believed that their cats enshrined the spirits of the dead, one reason why a white cat was carried with honour in the coronation procession of the young King of Siam in 1926.

The sacred cat of Burma is called Sinh, and the first of its kind belonged to the saintly Lama Mun Ha of the Lso Tsun Temple. He was the high priest of a cult that worshipped Tsun Kyanksie, a sapphire-eyed goddess who transmigrated the souls of dead priests into the bodies of sacred animals. Legend has it that the temple cat first showed the golden fur and vivid blue eyes characteristic of the Birman at the moment when it received the soul of the dying Mun Ha.

The particular temple of the Birman cat in Burma was the underground temple of Lao Tsun ('the dwelling place of the gods'), where the cats were believed by

Freya, the Teutonic goddess of Love and Beauty, in her chariot drawn by two cats.

the priests who served them to contain the souls of the faithful returned to the world after death. To the temple priests, these cats were gods.

China
One of the Chinese gods of agriculture, Li-Shou, was worshipped in the form of a cat. Peasants made sacrifices to this god after the harvest had been gathered in, hoping to ensure thereby the harvest's protection from rats and other vermin.

Chinese peasants knew to be wary of the cat, however. They believed it had the ability to recall souls from the dead – but as zombies. Thus, cats were kept well away from the dead before they were buried.

Japan
Cats, more protected in Japan than in other Buddhist countries, have a temple consecrated to them in Tokyo. This is the 18th-century temple of Gotokuji, in which cats are venerated after their deaths, for the temple is as much a necropolis as it is a place of worship. Around the altar, the great array of cat models have one thing in common – each cat has its right paw raised up to its eyes in the classic Japanese cat pose of greeting. These 'beckoning cats' are called Maneki neko. At the heart of the temple is the 'Spirit Cat', representing all the dead cats buried there.

Maneki neko, Japan's 'beckoning cat'.

Cats and witchcraft

The lives of cats and witches become closely entwined from the earliest times of mythology and folklore. Very great powers were attributed by ancient peoples to witches, descendants of the priestesses of the great Moon Goddess, Isis, Artemis, or Diana. Ovid tells us that Artemis changed herself into a cat when the Gods fled from Mount Olympus into Egypt, and Hecate, the dark aspect of Artemis and goddess of the underworld, also changed herself into a cat. Thus the connection between cats and the dark forces of the night and the underworld were clearly established.

One of the earliest witchcraft trials in Europe was that involved in the suppression by **Philip the Fair of France** of the old religious order of the **Knights Templar in 1307**. Many dreadful accusations were brought against the order, with 'confessions' to them being obtained under torture. It was alleged that the order had denied God and Christ, worshipped the devil, and practised sorcery and witchcraft. Satan himself was said to have presided over the Templars' midnight meetings, usually in the guise of a tom cat,

and that children and young women had been sacrificed to him. In truth, the Knights Templar were suppressed for political reasons: they were too powerful for the temporal rulers of the day to tolerate, and perhaps too worldly and sophisticated, too, beause of their long associations with the thoughts and beliefs of the religions and cultures of the Middle East.

In the suppressions of the three famous heretical sects of southern Europe – **the Manicheans**, **the Waldensians** and **the Albigensians** – in the 11th, 12th and 13th centuries (the last-named in horrifying massacres attending the crusade preached against them by Pope Innocent III), cats were involved. The Manicheans, a gnostic sect of disciples of Mani, a 3rd-century preacher from Babylonia, were accused of worshipping the devil in the form of a black cat; the Waldensians, a sect founded in Lyons by Peter Waldo, and the Albigensians, a sect in the south of France whose beliefs were derived from the Manicheans, were said to practise many evil arts, often in the presence of the devil who appeared to them in the form of a cat.

The first witchcraft trial of significance in England took place at **Chelmsford in Essex in 1566**, three years after the passing of the 1563 Act against witchcraft. Of the three women on trial one, **Agnes Waterhouse**, was hanged, the first woman known to have been hanged for witchcraft in England in modern times. Mrs. Waterhouse was accused of having received from another of the defendants, **Elizabeth Francis**, her pet cat Sathan, a white spotted cat which could turn itself into a toad and do many evil things. During the 15 or 16 years Mrs Francis had the cat, it was said to have carried out all manner of terrible tasks for her, for which she would repay it by giving it drops of her blood. (This business of the cat drinking its owner's blood, often mixed with milk, recurred in many other witchcraft trials.) For Agnes Waterhouse, Sathan was said to have performed numerous wicked acts, such as drowning the cow of widow Gooday and killing the geese belonging to another neighbour.

Witches' familiars, or spirits, in the form of cats featured in another notorious witchcraft trial held at the Chelmsford County Sessions, that of the **St Osyth Witches in 1582**. During the course of this trial, 13 women were indicted, ten of them accused of bewitching people to death. Amongst the accusations of bewitching, souring of wine, milk or curds, causing the death of farm animals and the like, which featured in the trial, were numerous accusations of witches having familiars or imps. **Ursula Kemp**, one of the two witches found guilty and hanged after the trial, was said to have four spirits, two of which were cats, a grey one called Titty and a black one called Jack. Two more of the accused women, **Alice Manfield** and **Margaret Grevell**, were said to have kept four imps, called Robin, Jack, Will and Puppet, all 'like unto black cats'.

At **Aberdeen in 1596** a group of women were accused of witchcraft and of assuming the likeness of cats

For many centuries it was believed witches could turn themselves into cats.

so that they could carry on their orgies round the town's Fish Cross undisturbed. The thought that the animals were real cats, drawn to the Fish Market by the smell of fish seems to have occurred to no-one – or, if it did, people were too afraid in the climate of the times to say so, lest they be accused along with the women. It is recorded that during the witchcraft craze which occurred in Aberdeen in 1596–7 24 men and women were burned. Among them was one **Janet Wishart** who confessed that she had sent nightmare cats to cause horrible dreams among her neighbours.

Another dispute among neighbours may have been behind the trial of **Isobel Grierson**, indicted on a charge of witchcraft at **Prestonpans in Scotland in 1607**. She was accused of attempting to make her neighbour, Adam Clark, and his wife and maidservant go mad through fear and noise, which she did by entering the Clarks' house 'in the likeness of her own cat, accompanied by a mighty rabble of cats'. The cats were said to have been accompanied by the devil, who pulled the maidservant's hair. More seriously, Isobel Grierson was accused of visiting another man, a Mr Brown, in the shape of a cat and inflicting a disease on him from which he later died. Mrs Grierson was burnt as a witch and her ashes scattered to the winds.

The most famous of all Scottish witchcraft trials was that of the **North Berwick Witches**, which ran on for two years, from **1590 to 1592**, and in which King James VI took a personal interest – as well he might, since at the heart of the trial was an alleged attempt to shipwreck and drown him and his Queen, Anne of Denmark, as they returned from Denmark to

The North Berwick Witches, John Fians, and a cat familiar.

Scotland in 1590. The trial grew out of the suspicions of a small-town bailiff about the night-time activities of his servant-girl, whom he tortured before handing her over to the authorities. She, in turn, began making all sorts of confessions about the unnatural practices she had been indulging in, dragging numerous prominent citizens into her sensational confession of a plot to kill the king. One of the accused, an elderly Edinburgh woman, Agnes Sampson, was interrogated in the king's presence in Holyrood Palace and another, John Fians, a schoolmaster from Saltpans, was tortured in front of the king in an attempt to make him confess to being the secretary of the witches' coven which had planned the plot.

Among the many confessions to crimes extracted from the people on trial, the most sensational was **Agnes Sampson's** story of how a gathering of nearly a hundred people, mostly women, had taken part in a black mass on Allhallows Eve and then sailed in riddles (sieves) to North Berwick where they had discussed how they might raise a storm at sea to wreck the king's ship. This storm, the most famous in the annals of witchcraft, was raised by baptizing a cat, tying the limbs of dead men to its paws and throwing it into the sea off Leith. Only King James' great faith, Agnes Sampson alleged, had saved him: it was stronger than their evil intentions. Agnes Sampson was hanged and burned. **John Fians**, too, after enduring dreadful tortures under which he continued to profess his innocence, was hanged and burned at Edinburgh in January 1591.

Margaret and Philippa Flower, daughters of a woman with a reputation for witchcraft, were tried and executed at **Lincoln in 1618** for the murder of the two small children of the Earl of Rutland, after they had been dismissed from the Earl's service. Philippa, confessing to the crime, said she had taken the glove of the

little boy, Lord Henry Rosse, from his home and given it to her mother, who had rubbed it on the back of her spirit cat, Rutterkin, before boiling the glove and burying it in the ground, so that Lord Henry should thrive no more. Sure enough, the boy and his sister died (probably, in fact, from a fever).

Matthew Hopkins, the 'Witch Finder General' who became notorious as a 'pricker' of witches in eastern **England in 1645–6**, caused many innocent men and women to be executed for witchcraft before public opinion, led by an indignant priest, turned against him. Again and again in the trials of Hopkins' witches, the accusation of having familiars was levelled against them. The familiar was usually some ordinary domestic pet, among which cats figured often. **Frances Moore**, one of the Huntingdon witches 'pricked' by Hopkins, confessed to having a white cat called Tissy who would lick the blood from pricks in her finger, after which she would curse someone and send the cat to him; shortly after, the person would die.

The **'Wapping Witch', Joan Peterson**, who was hanged at **Tyburn in 1652**, was said to have a black cat familiar. Joan Peterson confessed to having once bewitched a child while rocking its cradle after she had turned herself into the likeness of a cat.

At the trial of **Susanna Martin** at the Court of Oyer and Terminer in **London in 1692**, one of the witnesses was a neighbour, Robert Downer, who said that he had once accused Susanna Martin of being a witch, at which she had retorted that 'some she-devil would shortly fetch him away'. The very next night as he lay in bed, 'there came in at the window the likeness of a Cat, which flew upon him, took fast hold of his throat, lay on him a considerable while and almost killed him'. Luckily for Mr Downer, he remembered Susanna's threat and shouted at the cat to avoid him 'in the name of the Father, the Son and the Holy Ghost!' Whereupon, the cat leapt on to the floor and flew out of the window.

A witch-hunt in **Sweden in 1699** resulted in the executions of 15 children and the whipping of another 36 before the church door every Sunday for a year. The incident took place in the town of Mohra, where 300 children were accused of witchcraft. When examined, the children said that the devil had given each of them a cat, which had stolen butter, milk and other foods for the devil. The cats had also accompanied the children to the devil's palace.

The last trial for witchcraft in England took place in **Hertford in 1712**, when one **Jane Wenham** was found guilty of witchcraft, but pardoned. The only indictment brought against her was that she had conversed 'familiarly with the devil in the form of a cat', an accusation brought by a serving girl who had been having visions of the devil in the shape of a cat.

Witches were still executed in Europe for some time to come. **Sister Maria Renata**, a nun with a 50-year-long blameless record, was beheaded for witchcraft in **Bavaria in 1749**. The sub-prioress of a convent near Wurzburg, she had been accused of witchcraft by a

Classic depiction of a witch with her 'cat familiar'.

group of hysterical younger nuns. Under interrogation, Sister Maria Renata confessed, among many other sensational things, that the three cats she kept in her room were really devils in disguise and that they talked to her. It was her possession of these cats, said Sister Maria Renata, which finally caused her depraved life to be discovered. The church handed Sister Maria Renata over to the secular courts, who found her guilty and condemned her to death. Once she

had been beheaded, her body was thrown on a bonfire and burnt.

Modern witches are very different. An American male witch, **Mr Alan King**, recently interviewed in an American newspaper, said that he never attended orgies, knew nothing of casting spells and questioned the motives of people who did. He earned his living by selling incenses and oils, called Pagan Products, as aids to meditation. Despite this promotion of a new image, Mr King was photographed with his black cat on his knee.

Superstitions

Through the ages, people have believed that a cat's presence or its behaviour could portend many things.

In **Brittany** it was once held that tom cats should be killed when they reached seven years, or they would kill their owners.

The **Ancient Egyptians'** believed that the powers of a living cat could protect them from many kinds of evil, both natural and supernatural. A common form of jewellery among the Egyptians was the amulet, very often in the shape of a cat's head. Amulets would be left on the bodies of dead Egyptians, and a small ivory wand with the head of a cat buried with them, to help their souls ward off the many dangers on the journey to the Jalous Fields, where the dead dwelt.

In **Russia**, cats were put into a new cradle to drive away evil spirits from the baby that would be sleeping in it.

In many parts of **Europe**, on the other hand,it was believed that cats could suck the breath from sleeping children. The belief persisted up to our own time: Ernest Hemingway, living in Paris in the 1920s, was criticised for allowing his cat, F. Puss, to sleep in his son's high-sided cot. 'There were people who said it was dangerous to leave a cat with a baby,' Hemingway recalled in *A Moveable Feast*. 'The most ignorant and prejudiced said that a cat would suck a baby's breath and kill him.'

Many generations of **Englishmen** firmly believed that cats could turn milk sour and raise plagues of insects to destroy crops.

At the same time in many **European country districts**, cats were thought to be essential to a good harvest. In some places, cats would be buried alive in a newly planted field to encourage a good harvest. In others, less barbaric practices were followed by people believing in the wide-spread legend that there was a spirit or lesser deity who had made good corn its special responsibility. This corn spirit usually took the form of an animal, particularly a cat. At harvest time, special sheaves of

corn would be dedicated to the spirit's use, who was thought to remain in it until the time came for the next season's sowing, when the spirit would follow the seed out to the fields. In France, harvest's end was variously referred to as 'killing the cat' or 'catching the cat' or 'having the cat by the tail'.

Another 'seasonal' belief held about cats, generally in **Europe's Celtic fringe**, was that kittens born in May were not to be trusted, and ought not to be reared, lest they bring snakes into the house. The modified belief that kittens born in May made troublesome, badly behaved cats which would bring bad luck to their owners, persisted up to quite recent times. The belief is thought to derive from ancient Celtic mythology, in which the First of May, May Day, was sacred to Bile, god of Death. The whole of May was a month of ill-omen for Celts.

Many of the cat' activities have been seen as weather omens. Among the countries of **eastern Europe**, the belief persisted for centuries that lightning bolts were being thrown by gods or angels wishing to exorcise the evil spirits which were supposed to take possession of cats during thunderstorms; many poor cats found themselves thrown out of doors during storms so that their owners' houses might not be hit by lightning.

A cat sitting with its back to the fire was a sign of frosts on the way.

In **Scotland**, and in some other countries, a cat running about wildly and clawing at the furniture or floor coverings was a sure sign that high winds were coming. In the more remote parts of the Scottish Highlands, people were once said to draw a cat through the fire to raise winds to influence the course of ships at sea.

On ships, it was considered lucky to have a cat aboard, especially a black cat, though very unlucky to say the word 'cat'. Sailors used to see in any strange cat a disguised witch on board – presumably an extension of the ancient belief that witches would take the shape of a cat when trying to raise storms at sea. As on land, sailors would take the sight of a cat leaping about on the ship as a sign of approaching storms.

In **Germany**, it was held that two cats fighting near a sick man was an omen of death, while in **Normandy**, a tortoiseshell cat climbing a tree was portending the death by accident of someone nearby; a black cat crossing a walker's path in moonlight foretold death in an epidemic.

It was once widely believed that a cat leaving a sick man's house and refusing to return was a portent of the man's death. For others, a black cat coming and sitting on a sick man's bed was another portent of death.

Dreaming of cats used to be considered a very ill omen. Dreaming of a black cat at **Christmastide** could be a portent of a dangerous illness in the coming year, and dreaming that you are playing with a cat indicates that you should keep a sharp eye on your friends: they may seem fair but could be false.

The strange properties of the cat's eyes – the ability of the iris to change shape, and the way the eyes

shine in the dark – have led to some strange beliefs. In **ancient China**, people believed they could tell the time of day by looking at a cat's eyes.

In **Ancient Rome** it was believed that changes in the cat's eyes were connected with the changing phases of the moon. 'Though such things may appear to carry an air of fiction with them,' wrote Plutarch, 'it may be depended on that the pupils of her eyes seem to fill up and grow large upon the full of the moon and to decrease again and diminish in brightness on its waning.'

Cats' colours have also had special significance – and still do. It used to be considered a very good omen if a black cat walked into a house or on board ship; sailors' wives would keep black cats to ensure their husband's safe return. On the other hand, a witch's 'familiar', if a cat, was usually a black one. Black cats are still considered lucky in **Britain**, and a black cat walking in front of a bride and groom is seen as a particularly happy omen. White cats, on the other hand, are thought unlucky, white being the colour of ghosts. In **America and Europe**, it is generally the black cat who is taken to be unlucky, to the extent of 'having the evil eye', and the white lucky. In **China**, a black cat was long considered an omen of poverty and sickness. In **Japan** and other countries, a tortoiseshell cat is another lucky omen.

Another **wedding omen** concerns a cat's sneezing: a cat sneezing once near a bride on her wedding day was once considered a portent of a happy marriage;

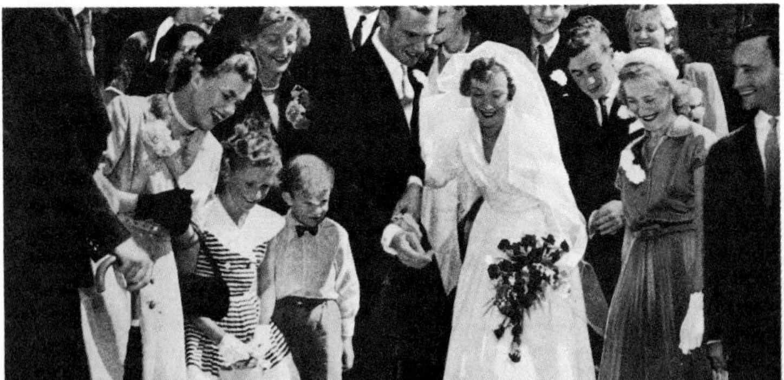

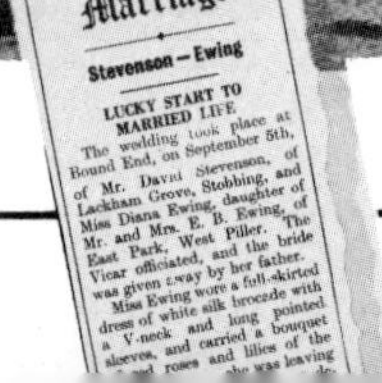

This English bride and groom are met by a 'lucky' black cat on the steps of the church. From the Picture Post, *20 Feb 1954.*

three sneezes and the whole household would have colds!

A cat washing itself in the evening was once taken as a sign that a friend would come soon.

And finally

YEAR OF THE CAT
The Chinese have given the cat a place in astrology for centuries. Each Chinese astrological year is assigned one of twelve animals, such as the monkey, the horse or the tiger. The last-named, often an inauspicious year from the point of view of war and other bad times, is followed by the Year of the Cat (sometimes called the Year of the Rabbit), which ought to herald gentler times: it does not always do so! Years of the Cat in the 20th century are:
1903, 1915, 1927, 1939, 1951, 1963, 1975, 1987, 1999.

SAINTLY CATS
Among the saints of the Christian church, three are considered to have the welfare of cats particularly close to their hearts: **St Jerome**, despite being depicted with a lion, is considered a good saint to evoke if a cat has strayed or been lost; **St Martha**, sister of Lazarus, and a patroness of those engaged in the service of the needy; and **St Francis of Assisi**, because he loved all animals.

FOND FAREWELLS
It is not uncommon to make memorials to our cats, as something to remember them by. The Ancient Egyptians created special cat necropolises; there is a cat temple and burial ground in Tokyo today.

In the Western world we tend not to go to these lengths. A pleasant resting place in the garden, with perhaps a named wooden cross to mark the spot, is as far as most of us go, though the Marquise du Deffand erected a splendid marble memorial, topped by a stone effigy of a cat, in memory of her pet early in the 18th century. A simpler memorial stone was put up by a vicar of St Mary Redcliffe's church in Bristol:

'The
Church Cat
1912–1927'

And **John Greenleaf Whittier** wrote a memorable epitaph for his Bathsheba:

'*To whom none ever said scat,*
No worthier cat
Ever sat on a mat
Or caught a rat:
Requies – cat.'

Or we might recall the epitaph to a cat called Perdita, quoted by Caroline Marriage in *Nine Lives*:

'When in ripe years she left us, her last feeble breath was a purr; and if the doors of Heaven are closed to such as her, I see no better hope for you and me.'

Acknowledgements

We wish to thank the following museums, institutions and individuals by whose kind permission the illustrations are reproduced.

Title Page: Shirar Snow Boots (owned and bred by Gerald and Stella Martin)
Cartoons on pages *12, 18, 24, 25, 38, 40, 43, 44, 49, 75, 79, 99, 124, 127* by Robert Heesom

Cats and Us

6, 8 British Museum; *11* Painting of Reverend Wenceslas Muff from *Cats Companion* by Jill and Martin Leman; *17* Mary Evans Picture Library; *19, 20* Both pictures courtesy of the Brontë Society; *20/21* Scottish National Portrait Gallery; *28* Photograph by Roy Beevers courtesy of *The Leader Series* (Bexley); *29* Courtesy of the PDSA.

The Inimitable Cat

30 Victoria and Albert Museum; *33* Animals Unlimited; *34* Guinness Book of Records; *35* Jeane Colville; *36* British Museum; *37* Dr. Ronald H. Cahn, The Gorilla Foundation; *41* Victoria and Albert Museum; *46* Courtesy of the Glenturret Distillery, Perthshire; 48 Photograph by Jim Dunn courtesy of the People's Palace (Glasgow Museums).

The Pedigree Cat

52 Photograph by Anne Cambers courtesy of Mr & Mrs G. Martin (breeders) and Mrs D. Cooke (owner); *53, 54/55* Courtesy of Sonia Halliday and Laura Lushington, *54* Animals Unlimited; *56* Jeane Colville; *57* Animals Unlimited; *58* (top) Animals Unlimited; (bottom) Himsay Sutepha, courtesy of Judith Jewkes, The Korat Cat Association; *59* Animals Unlimited; *60/61* Jeane Colville; *62* Courtesy of Suzanne Luff and Christopher Maud-Roxby; *63* Jeane Colville; *64, 65* Larry Johnson; *66* Animals Unlimited; *67* British Museum; *68* Both drawings Jeane Colville; *69* (top) Suzanne Alexander; (bottom) Pam Stephens; *70/71* Animals Unlimited; *72* Courtesy of the National Cat Club.

The Cat in the Language

81, 84, 87 Mary Evans Picture Library; *88* Courtesy of Vivian Noakes, author of *Edward Lear 1812–1888*, (Weidenfeld & Nicolson).

Cats in the Arts

91, 92 Tate Gallery; *93* Copyright reserved. Reproduced by gracious permission of Her Majesty the Queen; *95* The Bridgeman Art Library; *101* Courtesy of Hanna-Barbera Productions, Inc.; *103, 105, 106, 107, 108* National Film Archive/Stills Dept; *109* David Roberts; *111* The Illustrated London News Picture Library; *113* Courtesy of Peter Spurrier, Portcullis President.

Cult of the Cat

115 British Museum; *117* Mary Evans Picture Library; *118* Suzanne Alexander; *120, 121, 123* Mary Evans Picture Library; *126* John Frost Historical Newspaper Agency.

Colour section:

Bruce Coleman, Sally Anne Thompson, Spectrum.